MW01630508

Our Mission

Since 1964 the mission of The Foundation of American Christian Education is to publish and teach America's Christian history and method of education by Biblical principles to restore Christian self-government and character to the individual, to families, to churches, and to the nations.

The Foundation for
American Christian Education
Transforming the heart and mind of a nation

Renewing the Mind for Teaching and Learning

Self-Directed Study in the Principle Approach®
The Noah Plan® Curriculum

The Noah Plan®
Biblical · Classical · American Education

Renewing the Mind for Teaching and Learning

Self-Directed Study in the Principle Approach®
The Noah Plan® Curriculum

Carole Goodman Adams, Ph.D.
President
Foundation for American Christian Education

Elizabeth L. Youmans, Ed.D.
Author, "Self-Directed Seminar"

"The Principle Approach is a way of thinking and living by Biblical truth."
A parent of children in a Principle Approach school

The Foundation for American Christian Education
Chesapeake, Virginia

Renewing the Mind for Teaching and Learning

Self-Directed Study in the Principle Approach®
The Noah Plan® Curriculum

Copyright 2013 and published by
The Foundation for American Christian Education
Chesapeake, Virginia

ISBN 978-1-935851-08-0

First Edition 2004
Second Edition 2013

Includes the complete, revised
Self-Directed Seminar by Elizabeth L. Youmans
Originally published in 1997
by the
Foundation for American Christian Education
as part of
The Noah Plan Curriculum

Excerpts from
StoneBridge Standards:
Essential Practices that Produce Principle Approach Results
Copyright 2003, StoneBridge School
Used by Permission

Ordering and Catalogues:
The Foundation for American Christian Education
P.O. Box 9588, Chesapeake, Virginia 23321
800-352-3223 • FACE.net

Table of Contents

Introduction

Renewing the Mind for Teaching and Learning

Self-Directed Study in the Principle Approach®

The Noah Plan® Curriculum

That in the dispensation of the fulness of the times he might gather together in one all things in Christ.

—Ephesians 1:10

The Principle Approach is America's historic Christian method of Biblical reasoning which makes the Truths of God's Word the basis of every subject in the school curriculum.

—Rosalie June Slater

Teaching and Learning America's Christian History: The Principle Approach, Foundation for American Christian Education, 1965

The Principle Approach is a way of thinking and living by Truth.

—Parent of children in a Principle Approach School

Why We Suggest the Self-Directed Study

When we first began to teach our own children and those of our friends and family, the dazzling hope supplied by the Principle Approach made us bold to invest gargantuan amounts of time and resources needed to found a school. Among the many things we lacked as new school founders, the full understanding of the Principle Approach was the most remarkable and persistent. We knew our minds needed renewing and we sought help from many others who went before us. We were graciously taught, mentored, supplied, and encouraged to help us ultimately reach the goal. Our mission is to pass that help on to others who seek it.

What the Self-Directed Study Supplies

Because the Principle Approach is a new way of thinking today, it delivers a "renewing the mind" benefit that causes all of life and learning to be seen through a Biblical lens. The "renewing the mind" process is what puts many of us off onto an easier path. The renewing process takes time and, what's most exacting, thought. It is necessary to become a reasoner, "reasoning with revelation" as Noah Webster says, in order to attain wisdom. Reasoning is a process of study, applying principles and their leading ideas. Study takes time.

In the beginnings of our school, swept along by a robust and unfaltering hope, we looked every day into the faces of the children we taught for a reminder of the value of our investment. The love for our children inspires us to be renewed, to develop the reasoning necessary to teach them in the "nurture and admonition of the Lord." We are the guardians of the next generation, not just moms and dads, teachers and pastors. To fulfill our trust we must study, learn, renew, and reason so that we can invest good seed—what is true and right—so that our children will bring forth the good fruit God desires.

The Principle Approach® is the educational method upon which *The Noah Plan® Curriculum* is built. The Principle Approach® is a time-tested, age-old method of Biblical reasoning that causes learning to be reflective, master-able, and satisfying. It is the method employed during the era of the USA's founding that produced the quality of mind and character required to not only value liberty, but to design a governing structure that would assure personal and civil liberty for the first time in the history of mankind.

It is also a method abandoned by modern education. This fact explains the gradual slippage of personal and civil liberty in our nation, the creeping inroads of socialism in the thinking of our people, and the decline in character, morality, virtue, leadership, and the values once held sacred by our Judeo-Christian legacy.

The Self-directed Study is a first baby-step in the process of renewing the mind about education.

The Greater Goal

God loves to restore. What are the essential, uniting ingredients of any great work of restoration? Begin with vision. Without vision the people perish. We must be able to "see" the scripture being fulfilled *"That in the dispensation of the fulness of the times He might gather together in one all things in Christ, . . ."* (Ephesians 1:10) The vision is to restore to Christ what is His through education: the child, the subjects, the character, the results—bringing Christian liberty to the nation—and to the nations.

We offer this beginning step, *The Noah Plan Self-directed Study,* as a stepping stone to all who come after us to seek the way. We must possess the spirit of restoration, living out II Corinthians 3:17, *"Now the Lord is that Spirit; and where the Spirit of the Lord is, there is liberty,"* being full of grace and truth, having a learner's heart, understanding the nature of the battle, living like sons and daughters, and standing fast in the liberty wherewith He set us free.

The Mind Renewed for Christian Education

The mind renewed for Christian education is a mind that practices II Corinthians 10:5—"casting down arguments and every high thing that exalts itself against the knowledge of God, bringing every thought into captivity to the obedience of Christ." This mind is intent upon developing a thorough and inclusive Biblical worldview, internalizing the Biblical Principles of education and government, beholding Providential History and the Chain of Christianity® as the backdrop of every subject and every life, understanding the purpose and goal of education for the Kingdom of God, developing the Christian idea of the child, understanding the relationship between education and government, and possessing a living curriculum and its methodology in the Principle Approach.

Matching the Wine to the Wineskins

And no one puts new wine into old wineskins;
otherwise the new wine will burst the skins, and it will be spilled out,
and the skins will be ruined.
—Luke 5:37

The Biblical philosophy of education begets a fresh approach to both curriculum and method. The Principle Approach® enables the teacher to:

- ❖ Master the subject—its vocabulary, principles, leading ideas—the joy and spirit of the subject.
- ❖ Use methods that form Christian character and reason—the notebook approach, essay, debate, four R'ing, word studies, tutorial learning.
- ❖ Establish the purpose of learning—overviews, timelines, maps, goals.
- ❖ Create an appealing learning environment providing the right tools.
- ❖ Transfer the burden of learning to the student—teacher acts as governor, guide, inspirer, coach, exhibitor—the student produces the learning.
- ❖ Uphold consistently the standards of Christian scholarship and character—both the disciplines and rewards.
- ❖ Celebrate learning! Integrate music, art, dance, drama, instruments, song, pageantry, performance, photography—every visual and performing art—into the curriculum. Make whole days celebration days. Create traditions, awards, field studies, presentations. Celebrate!

The importance of education to the future of our liberty is a topic sadly lacking in these times. As Christians, we are accountable for the blessings of liberty God so graciously established in our nation with which we freely worship, send missions around the world, create wealth, establish homes and families, churches and businesses. The erosion of that liberty is the tragedy of this age. Our charge is to restore—to reclaim using the same means used to produce the first fruits of personal and civil liberty in the history of man—instilling Biblical principles of education and government in the characters and hearts of our children.

The education of youth [is] *an employment*
of more consequence than making laws and preaching the gospel,
because it lays the foundation
on which both law and gospel rest for success.
—Noah Webster, 1788

—Carole Goodman Adams

Part I

Renewing the Mind for Teaching and Learning

Self-Directed Study in the Principle Approach®

The Noah Plan® Curriculum

The Study Course for Restoring Christian Character and Scholarship to American Christian Education

Elizabeth L. Youmans

"To educate the children of today is to construct the foundation of the nation tomorrow. Faithless teaching makes for unfaithful citizens. . . . To save our country from the dry rot of secularism we are in need of a nation-wide education that honors God and that teaches study content in the light of God's Word."

—Dr. Mark Fakkema, Foreword
Teaching and Learning America's Christian History: The Principle Approach, 1965

The Noah Plan®
Biblical · Classical · American Education

Author's Preface

A MASTER TEACHER'S TESTIMONY

A pupil is not above his teacher, for everyone, after he has been fully trained, will be like his teacher.

—Luke 6:40

Dear Christian Educator,

Each of us can vividly recall at least one teacher whose influence, either positive or negative, left an indelible mark upon our spirit! As a child growing up in the Pittsburgh public school system, I had a music teacher, who believed in me and inspired me from the first grade through my high school graduation. A gifted and challenging individual, she encouraged me always to reach for a higher standard through her enriching music program. As an adult, God providentially placed two master teachers in my life. The first is Carole Adams, who saw something in my heart that my head had not discovered and called it forth! A visionary and master Principle Approach® teacher, she was used of the Lord to call me into teaching and to impart the philosophy of American Christian Education. The second is Rosalie June Slater, America's premier master teacher and architect of the Principle Approach, who has loved and often challenged me, while she mentored and taught me. They both continue as mentors and are now my colleagues here at the Foundation for American Christian Education. How blessed I am, and perhaps after I have fully been trained I might even be like them!

As the author of this *Self-Directed Seminar,* I have chosen to relate the inspiration and power of American Christian Education through my own testimony of seventeen years in Principle Approach teaching and learning, for I represent many thousands of American Christian educators who have walked a similar pathway of liberty in learning. I received my B.S. degree during the early 1960s, a time in America when liberal arts education was abandoned for the race to the moon! With a major in hospital dietetics, the thought of being an elementary classroom teacher never entered my mind. A decade later, when my own four children began entering the American public school system, I became very aware and alarmed that there was far more to education than what they were receiving. This triggered a search for the kind of education that produced not only disciples for Christ, but classic Christian scholars. By the grace and providence of God, our family became part of the founding of a Principle Approach school in Chesapeake, Virginia called StoneBridge School, when my husband and I enrolled our youngest son in the third grade.

God's call to teach includes His plan and providence for tooling.

I was astounded by Principle Approach education and greatly inspired by my son's American Christian history and classic literature courses. The first year I couldn't stay away from the classroom and volunteered to assist wherever they needed me. I yearned to know more about the rich curriculum and methods that produced such a spirit of liberty and joy in the teachers and children. (What I secretly desired was to be able to return as a third grader myself and start school all over again!) By mid-year I was asked to teach a biography of Abigail Adams to a class of first

©2013 The Foundation for American Christian Education

through third graders. With no college courses in education and few in liberal arts, I was certain I was not qualified to teach a Christian History Literature class! However, God had a plan for my re-education, one that dramatically changed the course of my life and allowed me to return to the third grade, as well.

Apprenticing with a master teacher imparts both the art and mystery of the craft.

Dr. Carole Adams, the founder of StoneBridge School, gently led and mentored me in the philosophy and Christian methods of Principle Approach® teaching and learning. I sat in her classes and observed her masterful teaching of history and literature. I was given a set of *Christian History* volumes, Webster's 1828 *Dictionary* and Rosalie Slater's Christian history literature *Teacher Guide* (syllabus) for the Abigail Adams biography. The syllabus guided my research and unlocked the rich curriculum of the founding and constitutional eras of America through leading ideas and Biblical principles—all very new to me!

Personally take responsibility for your re-education. Begin where you are!

My own re-education was underway, as the unknown world of America's Christian history, government, and education was unveiled to me. I discovered that teaching is both a science and an art. I spent several months preparing to teach, and now know that this was my Seminar in the Principle Approach. Like my salvation experience, teaching America's Christian history and government has revolutionized my life. I have been set free from the anti-Christian philosophies and the progressive methods by which I had been taught through the revelation of truth about education.

Begin a Christian History Study Group and consider and ponder together.

Our small faculty began a monthly Christian History Study using Miss Slater's course found in *Teaching and Learning America's Christian History* pages 303–366. Guided by leading ideas through America's Christian history and form of government, we studied primary sources, documented our understanding, and participated in lively group discussions, reasoning together.

Cultivate the habit of personal research and writing. There is no substitute!

The process of being retooled scholastically began slowly and steadily for me—one word study at a time, one principle at a time, one leading idea at a time, one link in America's Christian history at a time. I taught the students what I was learning. I used the methods and tools of scholarship with them which were still being refined in me. I developed lesson plans using my own God-given individuality, and God's Spirit empowered the children and me every day with great joy and a shared love of learning. By year's end, the students' STANFORD ACHIEVE-MENT TEST scores soared grade-levels above the national average. Real learning is lively, inspiring, refreshing, productive, and eternally rewarding!

Through summers of personal research and writing and school years of daily teaching and in-servicing, the years the locusts had eaten were slowly restored to me. The unfolding of God's Word conquered double-mindedness. As an elementary teacher, I developed and wrote curriculum for my classes. As an administrator, I was privileged to mentor other teachers. And now I consult and

©2013 The Foundation for American Christian Education

The key to success is Christian character.

The Hare and the Tortoise
from *Aesop's Fables*

A hare was continually poking fun at a tortoise because of the slowness of his pace. The tortoise tried not to be annoyed by the jeers of the hare, but one day in the presence of the other animals he was goaded into challenging the hare to a foot race.

"Why, this is a joke," said the hare. "You know that I can run circles around you."

"Enough of your boasting," said the tortoise. "Let's get on with the race."

So the course was set by the animals, and the fox was chosen as judge. He gave a sharp bark and the race was on. Almost before you could say "scat" the hare was out of sight. The tortoise plodded along at his usual unhurried pace.

After a time the hare stopped to wait for the tortoise to come along. He waited for a long, long time until he began to get sleepy. "I'll just take a quick nap here in this soft grass, and then in the cool of the day I'll finish the race." So he laid down and closed his eyes.

Meanwhile, the tortoise plodded on. He passed the sleeping hare, and was approaching the finish line when the hare awoke with a start. It was too late to save the race. Much ashamed, he crept away while all the animals at the finish line acclaimed the winner.

The Moral:
Slow and steady wins the race.

From the Bible:
"Let us lay aside every weight, and the sin which doth so easily beset us, and let us run with patience the race that is set before us, looking unto Jesus the author and finisher of our faith." —Hebrews 12:1–2b

assist educators around the nation and the world in implementing their expression of Principle Approach education.

Many Christian educators today have not taken time to reason and document their own philosophy of education. They race from the starting line into teaching, like the hare in Aesop's fable, not willing to proceed slowly and steadily along a reasoned pathway. Curricular materials are chosen with a view to spend as little time as possible preparing lessons. The "dead" curriculum, written from a secular worldview and "Christianized" with Scripture verses, lulls teachers to sleep, and they never reach the finish line of true Christian education!

I've been privileged to meet thousands of classroom and home educators throughout the years. Those who have the greatest success are those who look to Christ for the faith to develop their own curriculum and to write their own lesson plans. These are the teachers who become masters of subjects—the "lively textbooks"—and masterful teachers who model the character and standard of Christ in the classroom!

Sculpt your philosophy of education through this Seminar.

Therefore, before you race ahead to our curriculum, I strongly recommend that you take time and complete this *Self-Directed Seminar*. It is designed to enable you to:

- Appropriate the mind of Christ in education,
- Establish a Biblically sound philosophy of education, and
- Restore the character and scholarship in yourself that will support Christian education and self-government in your students.

Word meanings inspire ideas.

One of the distinctives of Principle Approach® teaching and learning is the use of an ennobled

©2013 The Foundation for American Christian Education

vocabulary in communicating principles and ideas. This is achieved through precise word usage which begins by defining words. Word meanings inspire ideas, particularly when defined from Noah Webster's 1828 *American Dictionary of the English Language,* the only English dictionary which contains Biblical meanings. *"The unfolding of your words gives light. It gives understanding to the simple. . . . Establish my footsteps in Thy word, and do not let any iniquity have dominion over me."* —Psalm 119:130,133

Word meanings inspire ideas that direct the pathway of our reasoning and thinking! When words are defined Biblically, they help us think and reason *with* the revelation of God's Word, freeing us from secularism. This enables us to *"take captive every thought make it obedient to Christ"* and appropriate *"the mind of Christ"* in teaching and learning.

Let's define our key words from Webster's 1828 *Dictionary* and light our pathway of understanding the Principle Approach®:

Principle: A *principle* is the cause, source, or origin of anything. It is that from which a thing proceeds, an element, a general truth, a seed.

Approach: An *approach* is the act of drawing near, an access. It is also a term used in fortification referring to both the advances made by an army, as well as the works thrown up to protect them in their advances.

Leading Idea: A *leading idea* directs one's reasoning down a specific pathway of thinking.

The Principle Approach is a Biblical manner of teaching and learning which places the Truths of God's Word at the heart of education. Please see the chart on page 86. This approach lays Christ at the foundation of all sound knowledge and learning and cuts through anti-Christian philosophies and methods of socialism and progressive education. It is remarkably like the education of the founding periods of America's history and restores this historic, Biblical model by placing God's principles at the heart of every subject and applying them to teaching and learning.

The Principle Approach is *education with a difference.* This "approach" to education is the best fortification and defense while waging the battle for the hearts and minds of this next generation of Christian leaders!

The Principle Approach produces the attributes of *The* Master Teacher within.

Be inspired and directed by your Biblical word studies as you plant God's principles of Christian education within. Be patient as they germinate and take root. Enjoy your research and allow that spirit to overflow into your teaching. The joy of Principle Approach teaching and learning is the liberty to govern your pace, the subject content you teach, and the enrichment you weave into your courses of study. Begin slowly and develop one or two subjects at first. Be compassionate with yourself! Nurture the attributes of Christ—*The* Master Teacher—within yourself! Cultivate the love of America's Christian history and government in yourself and in your students, and expect that Christian character and scholarship will be restored. Be confident that your educational vision for yourself and for your students will fully reflect Christ and His command to *"go ye therefore, and*

©2013 The Foundation for American Christian Education

Your commitment and choices will determine the consequences.

The Road Not Taken
by Robert Frost

Two roads diverged in a yellow wood,
And sorry I could not travel both
And be one traveler, long I stood
And looked down one as far as I could,
To where it bent in the undergrowth,

Then took the other, as just as fair,
And having perhaps the better claim,
Because it was grassy and wanted wear,
Though as for that the passing there
Had worn them really about the same.

And both that morning equally lay
In leaves no step had trodden black.
Oh, I kept the first for another day!
Yet knowing how way leads on to way,
I doubted if I should ever come back.

I shall be telling this with a sigh
Somewhere ages and ages hence:
Two roads diverged in a wood, and I—
I took the one less traveled by,
And that has made all the difference.

From the Bible:

"Make me walk in the path of Thy commandments, for I delight in it . . . revive me in Thy word. . . . And I will walk at liberty for I seek Thy precepts."

—Psalm 119:35, 37, 45

teach all nations!"

If you have unanswered questions or need more direction, please don't hesitate to telephone or write the Foundation for American Christian Education. We are here to serve you and we pray that you will walk in liberty of learning.

"Now may the God of hope fill you with all joy and peace in believing, that ye may abound in hope, through the power of the Holy Ghost."

—Romans 15:13

March, 1996

Elizabeth Youmans

Elizabeth L. Youmans, ED.D.

Call FACE for assistance.
1-800-352-3223 or visit FACE.net

©2013 The Foundation for American Christian Education

A SELF-DIRECTED SEMINAR IN THE PRINCIPLE APPROACH®

Let every student be plainly instructed and earnestly pressed to consider well, the end of his Life and studies is to know God and Jesus Christ which is eternall Life, Joh. 17:3. and therefore to lay Christ in the bottome, as the only foundation of all sound knowledge and learning.

—*New Englands First Fruits,* Harvard College, 1643

A Self-Teaching Course Seminal to the Beginning Principle Approach Teacher and Learner

With the dawning of the twenty-first century, this generation of young American Christians has a unique calling and a providential place in history. Just as Daniel and the three Hebrew youths of the Old Testament were *"called out"* from among their generation to lead in a culture riddled by occult practices and self-worship, in the same way our future leaders have need for an education that will also equip them to make unpopular choices, boldly confront pagan rulers and evil strongholds, as well as our nation's decline in every sphere with discernment, Godly wisdom, personal convictions, and a Christian work ethic.

The battle in which we American Christians are engaged is a spiritual and cultural battle for the hearts, minds, and souls of our youth. They must be strong in spirit, mind, and body so as to help solve, rather than add to the problems of the times. The need for this generation of Christians is to know God and His Word and through personal scholarship, under the Lordship of Christ, learn to apply knowledge in science and technology, in business and industry, in the arts, and in the economy and civil government. The need is to restore Jesus Christ, the Living Word, *The* Master Teacher, as the foundation for all sound knowledge and learning.

Principle Approach education is rooted in a philosophy of education that is unique to Christianity. Teaching and learning are natural functions based upon the individual value and worth of both the teacher and the student. Modern education has complicated the beauty of simplicity by mechanizing teaching and learning to the mass production of something that can only work when it is individual. A class cannot be educated. A subject cannot be taught. Teachers teach children, one by one, using the skills of *inspiring, cultivating, consecrating,* and *instructing*—believing the best for every child, calling forth his fullest potential in Christ. In order to accomplish such noble goals, the teacher must believe the best for *himself* as well, faithfully calling forth *his own potential in Christ.* Principle Approach education is rooted in these Biblical values and cultivates the attributes of *The* Master Teacher, Jesus Christ, within each educator.

Essential to your practice of Principle Approach teaching and learning is the completion of this Self-Directed Seminar. It is designed to establish your philosophy of education upon the Word of God. You will be reading and researching along a pathway of guided reasoning. The word seminar, whose root *"seminarium"* means to sow seed, is closely linked with the word *seminary.* A seminary is "a seed-plat or the ground where seed is sown, a nursery, a source of propagation." So begin thinking of this seminar as your seed-plat or nursery,

©2013 The Foundation for American Christian Education

a place where you will plant and germinate the seeds of Biblical principles for your philosophy of education. Your philosophy of education, in turn, will guide and direct every decision you will make pertaining to your teaching and learning.

How to Proceed

The Seminar consists of nine lessons with readings and written assignments. These assignments have been developed to assist you in completing the chart entitled *"Establishing a Christian Philosophy of Education."* Located on pages 98–101, this chart is for you to photocopy and record your personal research and reasoning, the "seed-plat" where you will sow and germinate the Biblical principles or seeds for your philosophy of education. The *Seminar* also includes a Glossary with definitions taken from Noah Webster's 1828 *Dictionary* that relate to teaching and learning.

After completing the *Seminar,* you will acquire a fresh vision for classic Christian education, and you will find yourself returning time and again to these Biblical principles and their applications, to guide and direct all your choices and decisions about teaching and learning.

Completing the readings and the written assignments are seminal to successful Principle Approach® teaching and learning.

The primary texts you will need for the Seminar are:

The Holy Bible—recommended edition for its providential view of history: New Analytical Bible, (Dickson Study Bible), KJV, World Bible Publishers.

American Dictionary of the English Language (1828), Noah Webster. F.A.C.E., 1967, 1965.

Teaching and Learning America's Christian History: The Principle Approach, Rosalie J. Slater. F.A.C.E., 1965.

Strong's Exhaustive Concordance of the Bible

The Christian History of the Constitution of the United States of America, Vol. I: *Christian Self-Government*, Verna M. Hall. F.A.C.E., 1960.

The Christian History of the American Revolution: Consider and Ponder, Verna M. Hall. F.A.C.E., 1975.

"The Christian Idea of the Child," Carole G. Adams; revised and republished in *Family and the Nation: Biblical Childhood,* Rosalie J. Slater. F.A.C.E., 2002.

If you do not have the F.A.C.E. volumes, they can be ordered from 1-800-352-3223 or www.face.net

©2013 The Foundation for American Christian Education

Lesson 1

Preparing for the Seminar

The Noah Plan®
Biblical · Classical · American Education

What's Wrong?	Let's Solve It!
American Christians have permitted secular educators to rob us of our rich educational heritage and the knowledge of our Biblical foundations!	Wake up and get armed with the educational philosophy that gave us our liberty. Take leadership!

Lesson 1 — Assignments

Readings

1. Lesson 1
2. Read pages xii–xxii, pages 52–57, and pages 88–89 in *Teaching and Learning America's Christian History.*
3. The books of Daniel, chapters 1–6, and First and Second Timothy. Make notes about their character qualities and any references pertaining to their education.

Reflections

Earnestly consider the following questions:

1. Do I have a teachable spirit?
2. Am I willing to rethink what I already know about Christian education and be retooled in Biblical methods of teaching and learning?
3. Do I like to read, research, and reason for myself and with my children?
4. Am I willing to expand my vocabulary of liberty and learning?
5. Do I enjoy writing? Am I willing to develop the necessary language skills to teach and correct student work?
6. Can I set aside perfectionism for excellence? Do I have the courage to persevere when my character is challenged?

Writing

1. Write a short summary of the characteristics of the education of young Daniel and Timothy. Apply to Christian education for the twenty-first century. Identify your role.
2. Apply definitions and principles gleaned from this lesson to your "Educational Philosophy Chart"; layout for photocopying found on pages 98–101.

©2013 The Foundation for American Christian Education

PREPARING FOR THE SEMINAR

. . . although we often succeed in teaching our pupils 'subjects,' we fail lamentably on the whole in teaching them how to think. . . . They learn everything except the art of learning.
—Dorothy Sayers, *The Lost Tools of Learning,* 1947

This Seminar is designed to take you on a spiritual journey, for thinking and reasoning with the revelation of God's Word are spiritual exercises. It's also designed to challenge you intellectually, to help you root out vain and deceitful philosophies, and to place you on a course of daily renewing your mind. When Jesus Christ was asked by a lawyer, *"Master, which is the great commandment in the law?"* He responded, *"Thou shalt love the Lord thy God with all thy heart, and with all thy soul, and with all thy mind. This is the first and great commandment"* (Matthew 22:36–38).

Loving God with all our mind is an intellectual exercise. For nearly a century, many American Christians have woefully neglected Christ's command to love God with all their mind. This has plunged America into our current crisis in education. Our nation is now called a "nation at risk" because of this crisis. Our watchmen have been asleep on the walls for decades. We have permitted secular educators to lead us astray and rob us of our American heritage of classical Christian education! Sadly, Christians continue to lose the battle of education because of ignorance and passivity! This Seminar is designed to awaken your mind and elicit a commitment from you to put on the whole armor of God and arm yourself for the battle!

From the writings of C. S. Lewis:

> "For every one pupil who needs to be guarded from a weak excess of sensibility there are three who need to be awakened from the slumber of cold vulgarity. The task of the modern educator is not to cut down jungles but to irrigate deserts. The right defense against false sentiments is to inculcate just sentiments. By starving the sensibility of our pupils we only make them easier prey to the propagandist when he comes. For famished nature will be avenged and a hard heart is no infallible protection against a soft head. . . .
>
> "And all the time—such is the tragi-comedy of our situation—we continue to clamour for those very qualities we are rendering impossible. You can hardly open a periodical without coming across the statement that what our civilization needs is more 'drive,' or dynamism, or self-sacrifice, or 'creativity.' In a sort of ghastly simplicity we remove the organ and demand the function. We make men without chests and expect of them virtue and enterprise. We laugh at honour and are shocked to find traitors in our midst. We castrate and bid the geldings be fruitful."
>
> *(The Abolition of Man,* Chapter 1)

©2013 The Foundation for American Christian Education

Distinctives of American Educational Systems

	Secular Public Education	Principle Approach® Education	"Modern" Christian Education
AUTHORITY comes from. ..	• The civil government (Federal, state, and local)	• The home, parents, and family	• The Church
The source of the PHILOSOPHY of EDUCATION is. . .	• Horace Mann, John Dewey • Socialistic principles	• Historic American Christian educational philosophy (Pre-Dewey) • Biblical principles • Individual conscience • Republican purpose, the character of Christ	• Fundamental reaction to Dewey and progressive philosophies • Evangelistic focus
The METHODS of teaching have these characteristics ...	• External stimulation • Behavioral modification • Free expression • Discovery learning • Reduced curriculum with lowered expectations and vocabulary	• Inspiring consent of the student to learn • Reflective thinking and reasoning from principles and leading ideas • The Notebook Approach and daily writing • Rich vocabulary of liberty • Tutorial method applied through the principles of: —Individuality —Christian character —Self-government —Conscience or property • Internal inspiration of the mind and heart • Student accountability for his own learning • Teacher is "lively" textbook—subject comes alive	• External control • Discipline • Content memorization and rote learning
The CURRICULUM emphasizes. ..	• Familiarity with subject content received in blurs, blobs, and bits • Memorizing and parroting facts • Multiculturalism • Social studies, language arts • Lowered expectations • God removed; man and his achievements glorified	• Mastery of principles and leading ideas of subjects to form a unity of truth • Teachers research and design their own courses • America's Christian history and government • Subjects valued and taught individually; their contributions to the Gospel identified • Classical literature, languages, and fine arts • Standard is elevated because the standard is Christ! • God and His wondrous works glorified	• Familiarity with subject content; cover the material to pass the test • Worldview of the textbook writer • Secular curriculum content "Christianized" with Scripture
The GOAL is...	• Socialization of student • Functional literacy • Democratic leveling	• "Furnishing each individual such aid as (education) can give to reach the fullest expression of his value in Christ." • Biblical Christian worldview • Christian scholarship and character for leadership/servanthood	• Christianization of student • Protection from public school influences • Literacy

The Noah Plan® ©1997 Foundation for American Christian Education

The Purpose of This Seminar

For as a man thinketh in his heart, so is he.
—Proverbs 23:7

American Christians have been searching for the type of education that builds classic academic disciplines, instructs in righteousness, and equips our youth with a Biblical, Christian world and life view! The ability of the Principle Approach® to restore Christian character and academic scholarship to American education, while discipling our next generation for Christian leadership in the twenty-first century, is now evidenced in thousands of educators and students around the nation. With its foundation rooted in the Biblical and colonial models of education, this approach provides a whole educational program that can be successfully implemented today by Christians around the world.

The primary purpose of this Self-Directed Seminar is to help you lay a solid foundation for successful Principle Approach teaching and learning by first establishing a *Christian philosophy of education* within you. Completing the Seminar will enable you to appropriate the excellence of Christ for your own scholarship and character by equipping you with the tools of Biblical thinking and reasoning. It also provides the opportunity for you to practice the disciplines of Christian scholarship and character, so that you can successfully teach them to your students. And the Seminar will introduce you to the principles, methods, and textbooks of American Christian Education.

Today most teachers and parents have received a *secular* education from *secular* schools and universities using *secular* textbooks through *secular* methods rooted in a *secular* philosophy of education. Most schools of higher education promote a *secular worldview* through the course content and the educational philosophy of professors, so that even Christian educators, to a large degree, must rethink and re-formulate their philosophy of education. Most Christian educators are unaware that their methods are secular and that the majority of Christian curricula and textbooks on the market today are produced using "traditional" curriculum "Christianized" with Scripture verses. Please read and carefully study the Chart—"Distinctives of American Educational System," on page 14.

For the committed teacher and parent, this means gaining the mind of Christ in education, searching God's Word for His standards and principles of education. It means redefining your own philosophy of education—that internal body of knowledge that governs your reasoning and guides decisions regarding education! It means being reeducated and retooled!

Our Challenge

Be what you would have your pupils be!
—Thomas Carlyle

A challenge is "a calling upon one to fight in single combat, an invitation or summons to decide a controversy!" The challenge for today's Christian educators and parents is to lead in advance of our students in the spiritual, intellectual, and cultural battle for their hearts and minds with an educational program that begins with truth, instructs in Biblical reasoning, and builds a "living curriculum" upon Christian character and conscience. Noah Webster, America's premier Christian schoolmaster, wrote in the March 1788 *American Magazine:*

> The education of youth [is] an employment of more consequence than making laws and preaching the gospel, because it lays the foundation on which both law and gospel rest for success.

The ability to reason Biblically is at the heart of individual and civil liberty. America was founded by "people of the Word," Christian men and women armed with truth, trained to govern themselves

©2013 The Foundation for American Christian Education

privately and publicly, and with a sense of domestic and civil duty. This historic record of excellence in education from our colonial and founding generations documents the Bible as its "first book of instruction."* The fruit of such an education was virtuous individuals, loving families (God's building blocks of nations), and a citizenry trained in the art of Christian self- and civil government. The challenge, then, is to revive this standard of education and to arm yourself with the mind of Christ in education.

The Required Commitment

Ezra prepared his heart to study the law of the Lord and to practice it, and to teach His statutes and ordinances in Israel. —Ezra 7:10

A *commitment* is "a pledge or a decision which cannot be recalled." The commitment of Ezra to Biblical education provides essential keys for us today in restoring our heritage of classical Christian education. Ezra, whose Hebrew name means *help,* was the religious and educational reformer who served with Governor Nehemiah in the restoration of Jerusalem after the Jews' Babylonian captivity. As the high priest and scholar, whom God also employed to compile the Old Testament Canon, Ezra restored true worship in the temple and God's Law to the people. He personally read the Word of God in the heart of Jerusalem's marketplace day and night (Nehemiah 8:8). After a famine of God's Law for nearly one hundred years, the Jews wept when they heard it and responded with repentance and fasting. Ezra led the educational reform that followed by raising the standard of God's Word on the battlefield of ignorance and illiteracy. The Jews returned to obeying His commands and restored His principles of education to their lives. From Ezra's writing we derive the process for his preparation as a high priest, a teacher, and a national reformer:

* Cremin, Lawrence A., *American Education, The Colonial Experience* 1607–1783, Harper & Row, Publisher, New York, NY, 1970, pp. 40, 60, 63, 587.

Step 1: Prepare Your Heart and Mind

Do not be conformed to this world, but be ye transformed by the renewing of your mind, that ye may prove what is that good, and acceptable, and perfect will of God. —Romans 12:2

All change begins internally with a renewed mind and a heart commitment. God creates us individually, calls us to Himself individually by name, and operates through His chosen individuals for His purposes and plan here on earth. The power for change in a republic resides in the individual. As an American Christian, it's up to you to face the challenge with faith, courage, and resolve! Begin with prayer, seeking the help of the Holy Spirit, the One who leads us into all truth. Then search the Scriptures to glean God's principles for education.

Step 2: Study God's Word

Study to shew thyself approved unto God, a workman that needeth not to be ashamed, rightly dividing the word of truth. But shun profane and vain babblings, for they will increase unto more ungodliness. And their word will eat as doth a canker. —II Timothy 2:15–17

The Bible is God's Handbook for His children and contains the foundation of all knowledge. As children of God, it should be our first book of learning, our primer, not only for spiritual instruction, discipline, and nurturing human relationships, but our first book of instruction in every subject.

The Principle Approach® has been called "reflective teaching and learning." This educational approach requires one to consider and ponder the purpose for everything in God's universe. Such reflection demands *time.* It also demands that we study and integrate God's Truths into our own lives and the lives of our students, as well as into the subjects we teach.

©2013 The Foundation for American Christian Education

STEP 3: PRACTICE GOD'S PRINCIPLES OF SCHOLARSHIP AND CHARACTER

A pupil is not above his teacher; but everyone, after he has been fully trained, will be like his teacher.

—Luke 6:40

Teachers have no credibility with students if they are not practicing what they teach. Begin to practice the four steps of learning and scholarship—research, reason, relate, and record. Identify and document the Biblical principles gleaned. Meditate upon them and give the Holy Spirit time to teach you what He wants you to learn. Apply these principles to your divine calling and use them as you begin formulating your own educational philosophy.

STEP 4: TEACH OTHERS

Whosoever therefore shall break one of these least commandments, and shall teach men so, he shall be called the least in the kingdom of heaven; but whosoever shall do and teach them, the same shall be called great in the kingdom of heaven.

—Matthew 5:19

With thorough preparation, thinking and reasoning skills retrained to begin with God's Word and an understanding of Christian methods for teaching and learning, by God's grace you are ready to begin your relationship in the classroom with the eternal hearts and minds of children.

©2013 The Foundation for American Christian Education

Lesson 2

Gaining the Mind of Christ in Education

The Noah Plan®
Biblical • Classical • American Education

What's Wrong?	Let's Solve It!
The secularization of our culture went to our heads! We've met the enemy and it is us! We are the products of the 'vain philosophies; of modern American education.	Restore your head as well as your heart to Christ! Learn to reason by Biblical principles and gain a truly Christian world and life view!

Lesson 2 — Assignments

Readings

1. Lesson 2
2. Read Hebrews 4:12. What are our defensive and offensive weapons in the Spirit?
3. Read Psalm 119, "the little Psalter within the Psalter." Identify and record the promises given for meditating on the Word of God.

Reflections

1. Study and reflect upon the vocabulary of education found in the Glossary.
2. Study the chart on p. 22 and the Word Study Format on pp. 23–26.
3. Become familiar with the steps toward Biblical reasoning.
4. Where is the battleground for believers?

Writing

1. Complete a Word Study for the word *renew*. Reason and relate Biblical principles in light of your study on education.
2. Apply definitions and principles gleaned from this lesson to your "Educational Philosophy Chart"; layout for you to photocopy found on pages 98–101.

©2013 The Foundation for American Christian Education

GAINING THE MIND OF CHRIST IN EDUCATION

And be not conformed to this world:
but be ye transformed by the renewing of your mind,
that ye may prove what is that good,
and acceptable, and perfect, will of God.
—Romans 12:2

Teaching and learning are natural functions based upon the individual value and worth of both the teacher and the student. Modern education has com-plicated the beauty of simplicity by mechanizing teaching and learning to the mass production of something that can only work when it is individual. A class cannot be educated. A subject cannot be taught. Teachers teach children, one by one, using the skills of inspiring, cultivating, consecrating, and instructing them in the basic skills of learning for a lifetime enjoyment and pursuit of knowledge!

What is Christian Scholarship?

Ideas form the basis of our worldview, the filter through which we channel experiences and ideas, rule or judge their efficacy, formulate thoughts, make decisions, and clothe them with words for communicating with others. Ideas begin in the mind, the seat of liberty or bondage, the battleground for our future welfare! The Apostle Paul, Biblical scholar of the New Testament, clearly understood the spiritual and procreative power of words, thoughts, and ideas and wrote the following to the church at Corinth:

> Now we have received, not the spirit of the world, but the spirit which is of God; that we might know the things that are freely given to us of God. Which things also we speak, not in the words which man's wisdom teacheth, but which the Holy Ghost teacheth; comparing spiritual things with spiritual. But the natural man receiveth not the things of the Spirit of God: for they are foolishness unto him; neither can he know them, because they are spiritually discerned. But he that is spiritual judgeth all things, yet he himself is judged of no man. For who hath known the mind of the Lord, that he may instruct him? But we have the mind of Christ!
>
> —I Corinthians 2:12–16

When working with young, pliant minds, it is essential for the educator to establish the habit of beginning the search for principles, answers, and solutions, in the Word of God, the *Logos*! It is the *Divine Word* that *consecrates* and *inspires* the mind and builds *intellectual virtue* and care should always be taken to glorify God—the source of all wisdom and knowledge! This is why Noah Webster, father of American education and scholarship,

©2013 The Foundation for American Christian Education

Basic Steps of Learning

Steps	The Definitions *Taken from Webster's 1828 Dictionary*	Educational Methods *Based upon America's Historic Record*
Research:	"To diligently inquire and *examine* in seeking facts and *principles*" *"Search the Scriptures; for in them ye think ye have eternal life; and they are they which testify of me."* (John 5:39)	Performing Biblical word studies by researching the vocabulary used and the Biblical foundation of the subject; Researching from primary sources; Gathering facts, rules, definitions, maps, charts, etc.
Reason:	"To *identify* the cause or ground of conclusion; that which supports or justifies" *"And Paul, as his manner was, went in unto them and three Sabbath days reasoned with them out of the scriptures."* (Acts 17:2)	*Deducing principles* from God's Word which produce moral rectitude. Outlining the subject; performing assignments requiring reasoning from cause to effect in essay format; produces abstract and critical thinking skills eventually leading to original ideas.
Relate:	"To tell or recite; to *apply* fact and *truth to life and knowledge*" *"Jesus saith unto him, I am the way, the truth, and the life: no man cometh unto the Father, but by me."* (John 14:6)	*Writing* definitions and deduced principles in *your own words*; writing out lessons learned and relating them to your own life; solving problems; performing experiments; taking tests; writing essays, speeches, theses, oratories, dramas, musicals; orally defending thesis.
Record:	"To *write* a regular, authentic, official copy for preservation of *what was studied*" *"And the Lord said unto Moses, Write this for a memorial in a book, and rehearse it in the ears of Joshua."* (Exodus 17:14)	Colonial copy books, commonplace-books, journals, personal and public correspondence, and official records reveal a Christian world and life view. Student's notebook work; essays, compositions and poems; theses; delivering speeches and oratories; debates; paintings; dramatic and musical performances.

©2013 The Foundation for American Christian Education

wrote the first American English dictionary and established a system of rules to govern spelling, grammar, and reading. This master linguist understood the need for precise word usage in verbal and written communication in order for our young nation to maintain her independence. Eager for Americans to be free from the bondage of Old World ideas, which were disseminated through our young nation's educational system, Dr. Webster carefully laid the foundation for a uniquely American education and the American usage of English words in his dictionary. He researched the root meaning of each word and defined each word in light of its meanings and usage in the Bible and in the new Christian constitutional republic.

Education is useless without the Bible.
—Noah Webster
Father of American Christian Education and Scholarship

Principle Approach® education has developed a valuable tool for inculcating the habits that lead to Christian scholarship in the Word Study. Each student develops the habit of research by beginning with God's Word through the Word Study, in which words are defined in light of how they are used in Scripture.

Word Study Format

The Word Study is more than going to a dictionary and defining a word. It is the tool of Biblical scholarship that places the student on the pathway of *reflective thinking* and *deductive reasoning* derived from the revelation of Scripture. The Word Study places the Truths of God's Word at the center of learning, which *illuminate the understanding* and *consecrate the mind.*

The *Word Study* is a tool for guiding the learner on a pathway of Biblical reasoning. In the *Word Study,* words are defined in light of how they are used in Scripture by using Webster's 1828 *Dictionary* and a Bible concordance. (Please see the model Word Study which follows on page 26 for details.) This process gives pre-eminence to the Word of God in deducing the Biblical principles of the subject and clothes the student's ideas with truth. This is the foundation upon which the pathway of *logical thinking* and *just reasoning* are established. It produces the *acquired* habit of Biblical scholarship and enables the student to reason from *cause to effect,* from *choices to consequences*—leading to a Biblical world and life view.

When practiced over a period of years, the student develops a *Biblical writing style,* references Biblical examples, and applies Biblical principles to problem solving. He is able to communicate his ideas in a logical manner and to persuasively express his ideas in a precise and ennobled vocabulary. And best of all, he has established the lifelong discipline of Christian scholarship based on a love of God's Word.

©2013 The Foundation for American Christian Education

These are the skills and habits that this generation of Christian youth must surely possess in order to overcome the failures of American education, the lure of their pop culture, and the deception of the New Age movement. Like Daniel and his three companions, our youth must be prepared to lead their generation as statesmen among the heathen and as prophets of the Most High God among believers.

Benefits Derived from the Word Study

1. Consecrates the mind;
2. Builds vocabulary (particularly one of liberty and Biblical government);
3. Increases reading comprehension and verbal scores;
4. Establishes precise word usage in written and oral communication (see *Perspicuity*, page 27);
5. Cultivates the habit of critical thinking;
6. Produces deductive reasoning skills (cause to effect—choices to consequences!);
7. Sharpens discernment of truth from error;
8. Inculcates a lifetime habit of scholarship;
9. Aids in establishing a Biblical world and life view.

Basic Tools:

1. A high quality three-ring binder
2. A good study Bible
3. Noah Webster's *American Dictionary of the English Language*, 1828
4. Matthew Henry's *Commentary on the Whole Bible* (for adults)

©2013 The Foundation for American Christian Education

Word Study Format

The Word Study reveals the Biblical meanings of words and unearths God's principles of knowledge and wisdom for application in every subject and sphere of life through the fours steps of learning. These steps are not ordered, but are used simultaneously to effect both Christian scholarship and liberty, as God's Truths become the internal property of the individual. Definitions are from Webster's 1828 *Dictionary.*

Research:	Reason:
Searching the vocabulary of the subject being studied for its source and purpose. *verb:* To search or examine with continued care; to seek diligently for the truth. *noun:* Diligent inquiry or examination in seeking facts or principles; continued search after truth. **Biblical Index:** John 5:39; Acts 17:11; 24:25; I Peter 1:10. **Method:** 1. A definition of the assigned word is written by the student in his own words. 2. Key words within the definition are identified and defined.	Reasoning from Biblical truths and identifying them in the form of principles to the subject being studied. Reasoning builds upon truth already researched. *verb:* To deduce inferences justly from premises. *noun:* A faculty of the mind by which it distinguishes truth from falsehood, and good from evil, and which enables the possessor to deduce inferences from facts or from propositions. **Biblical Index:** Isaiah 1:18; Acts 17:2; 24:25; I Peter 3:15. **Method:** Key words are identifed and recorded.
Relate:	**Record:**
Applying Biblical truth individually. *verb:* 1) To tell; to recite. 2) To restore. 3) To ally by connection. **Biblical Index:** Acts 18:26; Luke 4:27,32; Acts 19:1–4. **Method:** Personal definitions written by the student require that the student "relate" the word to his life.	The learner's written record of the study and application of Biblical truth. *verb:* 1) To write or enter in a book or on parchment, for the purpose of preserving authentic or correct evidence of a thing. 2) To imprint deeply on the mind or memory. 3) To cause to be remembered. **Biblical Index:** Luke 1:1–4; I John 5:10; III John 12; Revelation 1:1–3. **Method:** The individual's written work, filed appropriately in his notebook, becomes a permanent record of learning and is available for future reference.

©2013 The Foundation for American Christian Education

Sample Word Study

Please study the following sample. This is the manner in which you will want to complete your research and studies, in order to receive Godly revelation and leading ideas for application in your teaching and learning.

1. The word is defined from Webster's 1828 *Dictionary* and key words in the definition are underlined:
   heritage, *noun* [*Fr. from the root of heir.*]
   a) *Inheritance*; an estate that passes from an ancestor to an *heir* by descent or course of law; that which is *inherited*.
   b) In Scripture, the saints or people of God are called His *heritage,* as being claimed by Him, and the objects of His special care. (1 Peter 5)

2. Key words within the definition are defined:
   heir, *noun* [*L. haeres.*]
   a) The man who succeeds, or is to succeed another in the possession of lands, by descent.
   b) One who inherits or takes from an ancestor.
   c) One who succeeds to the estate of a former possessor. (Jeremiah 49; Micah 1)
   d) One who is entitled to possess. In Scripture, saints are called *heirs* of the promise, *heirs* of righteousness, *heirs* of salvation, etc., by virtue of the death of Christ and of God's gracious promises.

3. Relevant Scriptures are recorded:
   a) The Lord is the portion of my *inheritance* and my cup; Thou dost support my lot. The lines have fallen to me in pleasant places; indeed, my *heritage* is beautiful to me. (Psalm 16:5–6)
   b) Lo, children are an *heritage* of the Lord. (Psalm 127:3)
   c) And He gave their land as a *heritage*, a heritage to Israel His peoples. (Psalm 135:12)
   d) Thy testimonies have I taken as an *heritage* for ever: for they are the rejoicing of my heart. (Psalm 119:111)
   e) The Spirit itself bears witness with our spirit, that we are the children of God: And if chil-dren, then *heirs*; *heirs* of God, and joint-*heirs* with Christ; if so be that we suffer with him, that we may be also glorified together. (Romans 8:16–17)
   f) That being justified by his grace, we should be made *heirs* according to the hope of eternal life. (Titus 5:7)

4. Personal definitions written by the student require that the student "relate" the word to his life: "A *heritage* is property that passes from an ancestor to an *heir*. God called Israel His *in-heritance* or *heritage*. In the New Testament, God's people are His *heritage*. Therefore, I am called His child, His *heir*, and am a joint-*heir* with Christ."

5. Biblical principles deduced from the study enable the student to "take possession" of the word:
   a) Eternal life through grace is my *heritage* as a Christian.
   b) God's Word, the Bible, is also my *heritage*.
   c) As a Christian, I am God's *heir* and a joint-*heir* with Christ and, therefore, should govern myself accordingly.
   d) As an American Christian, I enjoy the *heritage* of Christian traditions and a system of law based upon the Bible. This is an *inheritance* from my earthly Christian ancestors that provides freedom for me to live as a child of God and to exercise my God-given rights in my daily life.
   e) I should guard and nurture my Christian *heritage* above all other possessions.
   f) I have a responsibility to share the Gospel, leading others to their eternal *inheritance* as a child of God.

6. The written record of the study is filed in the student's notebook for future reference and use.

©2013 The Foundation for American Christian Education

PERSPICUITY

Reading maketh a full man;
Speaking a ready man; and
Writing an exact man!
—Sir Francis Bacon, English Essayist

Perspicuity is that quality of writing or language which readily presents precise ideas to the mind of another. Noah Webster, the "man who defined America," acknowledged it as "the first excellence of writing or speaking":

> perspicuity, *n.* [L *per* and *speculum, a* glass.] Clearness to mental vision; easiness to be understood; freedom from obscurity or ambiguity; that quality of writing or language which readily presents to the mind of another the precise ideas of the author.

Preciseness of language is essential in good communication and certainly one of the basic tools needed in the "art and mystery" of teaching! Mastering the vocabulary of a subject lays the foundation for understanding the subject being studied. It aids in guiding the pathway of thinking and reasoning because words inspire ideas.

Ambiguous and imprecise word usage is one of the enemy's most effective tools for conveying confusion and misunderstanding in thinking, reasoning, and communication. Contemporary dictionaries in common usage in American educational institutions have obscured or removed Biblical word meanings. Its fruit is evident in the high rate of illiteracy and fallacious reasoning in our society. The value of using Noah Webster's original dictionary is that he researched the etymology of words based upon their usage in Scripture—the eternal Light, the source of illumination for the mind.

This method of study builds Biblical scholarship and provides the pathway for understanding and correct reasoning! In order to think precisely about "thinking and reasoning," it is essential to use the critical vocabulary of the subject.

It is also essential to use an accurate translation of the Bible. In building perspicuity, it is worth noting that many translations are on the market that have been "dumbed-down" and use ambiguous language, which in many cases have obscured original meanings of words. For example, the popular *New International Version* (NIV) is written at a fifth grade reading level. The 1611 *Authorized King James Version,* with its lyric beauty and scholastic integrity, represents the flowering period of our English language and is written at a twelfth grade reading level.

Mastering the vocabulary of a subject is the first step in taking possession of it and becoming a master of the subject. Word meanings inspire ideas, as well as convey a philosophy of government.

Perspicuity is the key to artful communication. In order to fulfill the great commission, we must be able to articulate ideas and teach others. Reading with comprehension, speaking with readiness, and writing with precision and persuasion are all marks of the Christian scholar.

Go therefore and make disciples of all the nations . . .
teaching them to observe all that I commanded you.
—Matthew 28:19–20

©2013 The Foundation for American Christian Education

Lesson 3

The Notebook Approach

The Noah Plan®
Biblical · Classical · American Education

What's Wrong?	Let's Solve It!
Consumerism has consumed us! Modern education is a consumer-driven industry cranking the gears of functional illiteracy!	Classic Principle Approach® education makes the learner a producer and establishes the skills and character of scholarship through the Notebook Approach.

LESSON 3 — ASSIGNMENTS

READINGS

1. Lesson 3
2. Read pp. 88–102 in *Teaching and Learning America's Christian History*.
3. Reflect upon the notebook standard and the Notebook Grading Sheet on pp. 34–35. Consider how you can adapt the Grading Sheet for the various grade levels of learning.

REFLECTIONS

1. Study the chart on p. 33 entitled "Comparison of Two Educational Approaches." Highlight and note the many suggestions for methods and curriculum writing on your "Educational Philosophy Chart."

WRITING

Apply definitions and principles gleaned from this lesson to your "Educational Philosophy Chart"; layout for you to photocopy found on pages 98–101.

©2013 The Foundation for American Christian Education

THE NOTEBOOK APPROACH

Reading maketh a full man;
Speaking a ready man; and
Writing an exact man!
—Sir Francis Bacon, English Essayist

The Notebook Approach is both the *tool* and the primary *method* used in the Principle Approach® for establishing Christian scholarship in both teaching and learning. It embraces the four steps of learning—RESEARCH—REASON—RELATE—RECORD—commonly called "the Four R's." Centuries old, it is the excellent method found in the educational background of the greatest thinkers and leaders in history. In the Bible alone, hundreds of references to writing, making records, books, and chronicles are found. Mastery of learning requires that the student make a written record of his study, and the more detailed and exacting the record, the greater the mastery attained. It can easily be concluded that as the adherence to historical standards and methods, including notebook writing, declined in American education, quality and excellence diminished.

The Notebook Approach is more than an efficient way of filing the learner's work in a three-ring binder, which is how it appears to the new educator and student. If that were all it embraced, teachers would not spend the immense labor and time that the Notebook Approach requires in teaching and learning, particularly at the primary level of learning. However, the Notebook Approach is a valuable tool of reasoning and academic discipline that produces Christian scholarship and a Biblical world and life view in both the teacher and student.

As each learner applies the Notebook Approach to his personal research and study, the real value of the notebook becomes apparent. As he takes possession of the subject, it liberates both teacher and student to become *active producers* rather than *passive consumers* in the educational process. The burden and accountability for learning is placed upon each individual. The teacher or student who learns to reason from principles and leading ideas gleaned from personal research and reasoning, eventually becomes a master of. subjects. He is equipped for life with a self-governing character, an independent mentality, and the Christian work ethic. Please read and study the chart *"Comparison of Two Educational Approaches"* on page 33.

The Notebook Approach is both *spirit* (internal or cause) and *letter* (external or effect). As in most other learning experiences, the teacher's understanding of the Notebook Approach begins with the concrete and slowly moves to the abstract. The concrete aspect of this method of teaching and learning consists of three-ring binders, dividers, title pages, the giving of notes on the chalkboard to be laboriously copied into the designated section of the notebook, the grading, correcting, and filing of papers. If the concrete aspect was all—both end and goal—the Notebook Approach would be just a form unworthy of the labor it requires, and a well organized, discriminating textbook would serve as well. It is easy to become entrapped in serving the letter and miss the spirit of this valuable tool.

©2013 The Foundation for American Christian Education

The Value of the Notebook Approach

1. It aids in the Biblical purposes of education by "enlightening the understanding, correcting the temper, and forming the habits of youth that fit him for usefulness in his future station." (Webster's 1828 *Dictionary*)
2. It is the product of the student's creativity and illustrations.
3. It is a permanent record of his productivity.
4. It aids his parents and teacher in his progress, showing exactly what is being taught. It shows graphically his character development, his industry, diligence, and responsibility.

What makes the Notebook Approach a useful and extremely valuable instrument of education is when each teacher applies the method to his personal research and study. As he takes possession of the subject, it sets him free to become the "living textbook"—the talking, acting, responding textbook, able to call forth true learning from individual students. As a "master" of his subject, he is able to be more flexible, spontaneous, and inspirational in the classroom. Not tied to a "dead" textbook or a teacher manual, his fresh lessons and instructions touch the heart of every child in the classroom.

Combined with the structure of discipline and habits of work skills that the Notebook Approach requires, the student becomes involved with the subject as he "Four R's," thinking and reasoning, writing his thoughts, making a record of his study. He grows in his responsibility for his own learning, building strong qualities of character. The Notebook Approach is the tool of reasoning and academic discipline that restores academic excellence to education and forms individuals whose characters enable them to achieve their God-given potential and accomplish great moral feats!

George Washington left us a record of his early learning. His childhood copybooks, beginning at age thirteen, are stored in the Library of Congress. Jared Sparks, author of *The Life of George Washington*, 1855, wrote this account of Washington's notebooks:

> . . . His manuscript and schoolbooks, from the time he was thirteen years old, have been preserved. He had already mastered the dif-ficult parts of arithmetic and these books begin with geometry. . . . The manuscripts fill several quires of paper and are remarkable for the care with which they were kept, the neatness and uniformity of the handwriting, the beauty of the diagrams, and a precise method and arrangement in copying out tables and columns of figures.

The sample at the right is from young Washington's geometry copybook. The date at the top of the page is August 15, 1745.

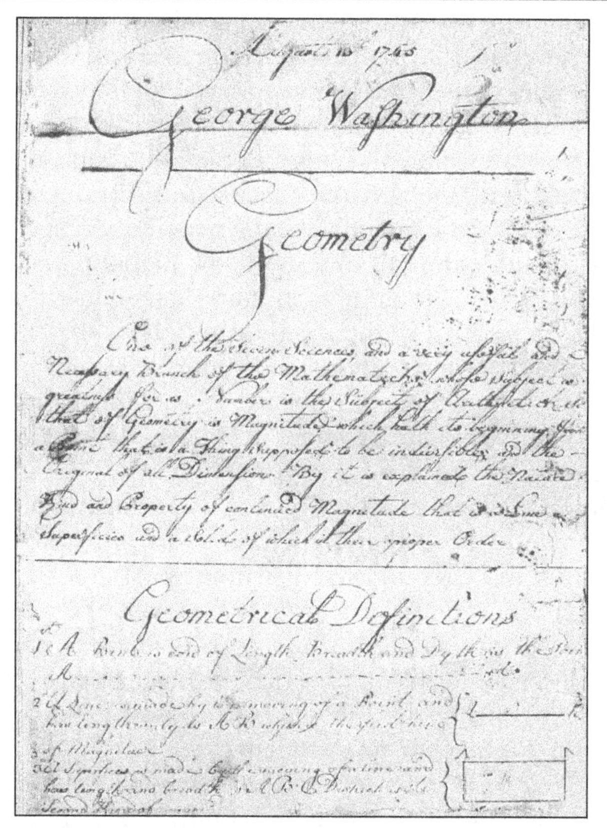
August 15th 1745
George Washington
Geometry
Geometrical Definitions

©2013 The Foundation for American Christian Education

Comparison of Two Educational Approaches

The Workbook Approach *Conditioned Learning* *Consumer-Oriented* Result: *Dependent Character*	The Notebook Approach *Reflective Learning* *Producer-Oriented* Result: *Independent Character*
1. Curriculum is structured by the pursuit of information and its regurgitation. Glorifies man and his knowledge! 2. Discourages original thinking through true-false, fill-in-the-blank, one-word responses. 3. Produces no record of learning—papers discarded, workbooks destroyed. Student has no sense of "value" for the effort. Parents not certain what is being taught. 4. Subject is not the internal property of the student. Information quickly forgotten! Language must be "dumbed down" for understanding. Communication is vague. Student often unable to give meaningful answers. 5. Produces the ability to take short answer tests with a "recognition" mentality. Students parrot back the "right" answers for the "A" on the test. 6. Has no standard of Christian scholarship or work ethic—no accountability for learning! 7. Discourages a lifetime enjoyment of learning. 8. The burden of learning rests on the teachers! 9. Teachers are tied to teacher manuals and canned curriculum content—someone else's ideas and lesson plans. 10. Fosters opportunities of irresponsibility, ignorance, illiteracy, inertia—a slavish, dependent mentality and character—a liberal, socialistic, secular world and life view!	1. Curriculum is structured by Biblical *principles* and *leading ideas*. Glorifies *God* as the author of the subject! 2. Encourages *mastery* of subjects. Students research. Required to *write* complete thoughts, sentences, paragraphs, essays. 3. Produces a *permanent record* of learning. Student values his labor and is able to refer back to his study. Parents see exactly what is being taught and required daily, as well as the child's progress. 4. Student takes command of the subject and it becomes his personal property. Must be able to reason and think critically; acquires the ability to articulate with *perspicuity*—speak and write with the mastery and authority of God's Word. 5. Produces *reflective* understanding. Essay tests require an understanding of principles and concepts. Students reason for themselves, solve problems. 6. Holds student to the standard *of excellence* in Christ. He practices Christian scholarship. 7. Produces "philomaths"—those who love learning and pursue a lifetime of study. 8. The burden of learning rests on the student! 9. Teacher becomes the *lively textbook,* the living epistle in the classroom, by researching and developing his own curriculum and lesson plans. 10. Fosters opportunities for individuality, industry, productivity, accountability, reasoning, mastery of knowledge—a *self-governing, independent* mentality and character—a conservative, Biblical, Christian world and life view!

©2013 The Foundation for American Christian Education

The Notebook Method

The notebook standard of form is taught at the beginning of each year and reinforced by the teacher daily.

Binders:

Purchase good quality binders and group several subjects in the same two and two-and-a-half-inch binder. For example:

Notebook 1: Bible, History, and Geography
Notebook 2: English, Reading, and Latin
Notebook 3: Science, Arithmetic, and P.E.
Notebook 4: Literature, Art, Music, and French

Label each binder with the child's name and the subjects. Students should be taught to steward their notebooks with care.

Set-Up:

Dividers: Have students provide notebook dividers and label them in class. Each subject is unique and will require an individual setup form. Suggested format:

- History dividers: *History Research, History Reason,* and *History Relate*
- English dividers: *Orthography, Grammar, Composition, Speech,* and *Syntax*
- Literature dividers: *Introduction, Bible as Literature, Poetry, Shakespeare,* plus the titles of individual classics being taught.

Title Page: Just as every book has a title and a copyright page, a title page should be made for each subject with the following information and perhaps a suitable quote and illustration, (see example above right).

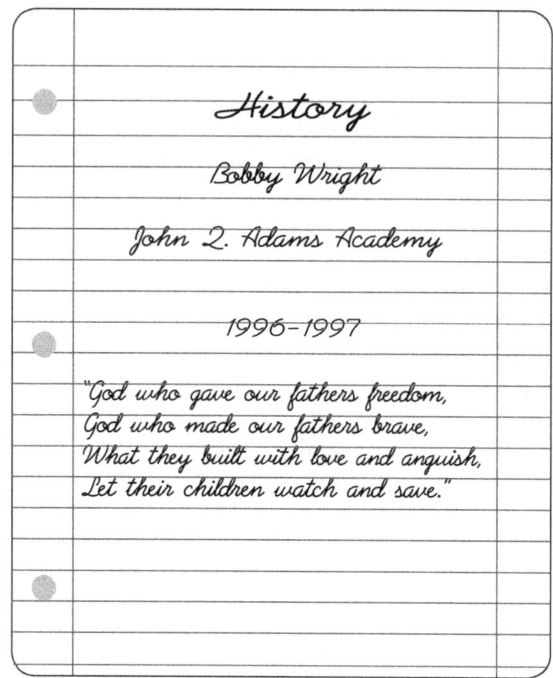

Sample Title Page

Classroom Constitution: Place the classroom constitution behind the title page. See page 36.

Notebook Grading Sheet: The four-fold standard of neatness, accuracy, completeness, and order is periodically graded through the year and averaged into the quarterly grade given on the students' report cards. The notebook grade, therefore, is a grade for work skills and character more than for academic ability. This provides for a measurement of the whole purpose of education: "correcting the temper, forming manners and habits, fitting for usefulness," as well as "enlightening the mind." In elementary school, the notebook grade is generally weighted one-third of the subject grade. The notebook grading sheet is placed after the classroom constitution. See sample on page 35.

The Subject Overview: The subject overview is written by the teacher and is a tool of communication for parents, as well as students, relating the course objectives, content, resources, routines, and projects. (See the *Noah Plan® Lessons* books for each grade. See pages 95–96 herein for "How to Use *The Noah Plan*.")

Storage:

Build adequate shelving in the classroom to house each student's notebooks, dictionary, atlas, and Bible. Plastic crates screwed to shelves provide durable individual storage units.

©2013 The Foundation for American Christian Education

NOTEBOOK GRADING SHEET

Student ______________________ Grade ______________________

Teacher ______________________

Subject ______________________

Neatness (25 Points) A. Margins B. Penmanship C. Tabs	**Order (25 Points)** A. Dividers B. Notes C. Assignments & Tests
Accuracy (25 Points) A. Copying B. Corrections Completed	**Completeness (25 Points)** A. Preliminary Pages B. Notes C. Assignments

Total Notebook Grade

Grade: **Comments:**

1st Grading Period: _____ ______________________________

2nd Grading Period: _____ ______________________________

3rd Grading Period: _____ ______________________________

The Noah Plan®

Biblical • Classical • American Education

©2013 The Foundation for American Christian Education

CLASSROOM CONSTITUTION

We, the students and teacher of the ____________ Grade Class, in order to:

(1) form a more perfect classroom, (2) establish just rules, (3) insure peace, (4) promote the general good of each student, and (5) secure the blessings of liberty, do establish this Constitution for governing ourselves at school.

Each individual in our classroom will pledge:

I choose to put God first in my life and to daily ask for His help in governing myself by "walking in the Spirit." (Galatians 5:22–25, Romans 8:1)

I will be prepared to begin each day with all books, notebooks, papers, pencils, and assignments ready.

I will be respectful of teachers and classmates. I will remember to be quiet in the hallways and to lower my voice in the lunchroom.

I will remain attentive and speak only with permission.

I will be a good steward of my property, as well as the property of others. I will be a good steward of my time, using it wisely.

____

Signature of Student

As your teacher, I will guard your individuality, liberty, and safety for the benefit of all.

____

Signature of Teacher

©2013 The Foundation for American Christian Education

Lesson 4

Education

A Whole View

The Noah Plan®

Biblical · Classical · American Education

What's Wrong?	Let's Solve It!
When you don't know where you're going, any road will get you there!	Get a vision of the end goal and aim for it!

LESSON 4 — ASSIGNMENTS

READINGS

Lesson 4

REFLECTIONS & WRITING

1. Begin your Biblical study of education by completing Word Studies on the following words from the definition of education:
   - instruction
   - discipline
   - understanding
   - the four *active* verbs in the definition
   - habit
   - art
   - science

2. In the light of God's Word, build your reasoning and thinking upon the following questions:
   - Who is God? What are the characteristics of His nature?
   - What is the nature of man?
   - Why does man need a Savior?
   - What is the role of parents in education?
   - What is the role of the teacher?
   - What is America's Christian heritage in education?
   - What is the fruit of American Christian education?
   - How will you evaluate education?

3. Using the chart for "Establishing a Christian Philosophy of Education," pp. 98–101, identify and write the qualities and principles for the Leading Ideas on the chart. This exercise, although it will take time and reflective thought, is the most important step toward renewing your mind concerning education and establishing your own definition and philosophy of education.

©2013 The Foundation for American Christian Education

EDUCATION—A WHOLE VIEW

All scripture is given by inspiration of God,
and is profitable for doctrine, for reproof,
for correction, for instruction in righteousness,
that the man of God may be complete,
thoroughly equipped for every good work.
—II Timothy 3:16–17

Definition of Education:

It is extremely important to thoroughly understand the meaning of education from a Biblical Christian worldview. Noah Webster, father of American education and scholarship, was a master philologist who defined words by researching their root meanings in the original languages and in the Bible. His *American Dictionary of the English Language* (1828) is a valuable and one-of-a-kind study tool for all American Christians. His definition of education should be memorized by all pastors, parents, and educators:

> education, noun, [*L. educatio*].
> The bringing up, as of a child; instruction; formation of manners. *Education* comprehends all that series of instruction and discipline which is intended to enlighten the understanding, correct the temper, and form the manners and habits of youth, and fit them for usefulness in their future stations. To give children a good *education* in manners, arts and science, is important; to give them a religious *education* is indispensable; and an immense responsibility rests on parents and guardians who neglect these duties.

Compare this definition of education with the definition from any contemporary dictionary.

Christian education requires that God's covenant people place His commands and precepts at the heart of teaching and learning. This develops our ability to reason with the revelation of God's Word as a habit of learning. A search of the Scriptures reveals that a true educational experience for God's people was meant to be an *education with a difference!* It has at its heart the *standard of holiness* —of separation from all other peoples in order to wholly belong to God. The Book of Leviticus is the "book of holiness" and contains God's commands for holy living. *And the Lord spake unto Moses, saying, Speak unto all the congregation of the children of Israel, and say unto them, Ye shall be holy: for I the Lord your God am holy.* (Leviticus 19:1–2)

The object and aim of this kind of education are the knowledge of God and submission to the authority of His Divine Word. When God's Living Word is at the heart of education, it produces the following:

1. Renews and consecrates the mind;

2. Illumines the pathway of thinking and reasoning;

3. Reveals God's principles and purpose for every subject;

©2013 The Foundation for American Christian Education

4. Provides the methods by which they will be imparted;

5. Builds a Biblical Christian world and life view based upon the presuppositions of the Bible within the student.

Gaining the Mind of Christ in Education

"As ye have therefore received Christ Jesus the Lord, so walk ye in him: rooted and built up in him, and stablished in the faith, as ye have been taught, abounding therein with thanksgiving. Beware lest any man spoil you through philosophy and vain deceit, after the tradition of men, after the rudiments of the world, and not after Christ. For in Him dwelleth all the fulness of the Godhead bodily. And ye are complete in Him."

—Colossians 2:6–10a

The word *philosophy* comes from the Latin root which means "to love wisdom." It is defined as the reason or cause of things; the body of wisdom, laws, or principles which govern all the subordinate phenomena in any department of knowledge. (Webster's 1828 *Dictionary*) Your philosophy of education is the internal body of wisdom that governs all educational choices, decisions, policies, and methods for instruction and discipline. It affects who will teach, choice of curriculum, school governance, classroom discipline, student programs, and the fruit produced by each individual student.

An educational philosophy contains the "seeds" that are to be planted and the means by which to cultivate them in the hearts and minds of children. If you want an oak tree to grow, you must first plant an acorn. The same is true for education. Just having Christian teachers in the classroom and gluing Scripture verses to secular curriculum do *not* produce Christian education or graduates with a Christian worldview.

Your philosophy of education should be rooted in the authority of God's Word. The Apostle Paul vigorously warned first century Christians many times to beware of the spirit of the antichrist, the vain philosophies of the world's system after the tradition of men, lest their minds be taken captive through deception and they be led astray! Memorize the following Scriptures and apply them to our life:

- *Casting down imaginations, and every high thing that exalteth itself against the knowledge of God, and bringing into captivity every thought to the obedience of Christ.* —II Corinthians 10:5

- *But I am afraid that as the serpent deceived Eve by his craftiness, your minds will be led astray.* —II Corinthians 11:3

- *And be not conformed to this world: but be ye transformed by the renewing of your mind, that ye may prove what is that good, and acceptable, and perfect, will of God.* —Romans 12:2

- *See to it that no one takes you captive through philosophy and empty deception, according to the tradition of men, according to the elementary principles of the world, rather than according to Christ.* —Colossians 2:8

Please read the chart, "Rudimentary Pagan versus Christian Views" on the following page.

©2013 The Foundation for American Christian Education

Rudimentary Pagan versus Christian Views

Pagan	Christian
Views of Man	
1. Man is simple, primitive, but becoming better. 2. Human progress is in altering external environment to produce better internal character. 3. The effect: Man is in bondage to his environment.	1. Man is fallen and needs a Savior. 2. Human progress is in altering the internal nature/character to produce a better environment. 3. The effect: Free, independent, self-governing individual.
Views of History	
1. All things came into being through chance happenings. 2. Human progress is in altering external environment to produce better internal character. Man's environment is the cause of man's actions. 3. The goal is to change society economically, politically, etc. 4. Success is in the ability to adapt and to adjust to society. 5. The purpose of history is man's story and man's glory.	1. All things were created by God. (John 1:3) 2. Man's heart is the cause of his actions. (Mark 7:20–23) 3. The goal is to become a new creation. (II Corinthians 5:17) 4. Success is in overcoming through Christ. (Joshua 1:8; I John 4:4) 5. Purpose of history: God's story and glory.
Views of Education	
1. Evolutionary 2. Human progress is in altering external environment to produce better internal character. Exerts external influences by— • stimulating (subject) • motivating (consume) • enculturating (conform) • indoctrinating (confuse) —*Making environment the cause* 3. The effect: Control the individual by changing behavior.	1. Wholistic (John 1:3) 2. Appeals to the internal by— • inspiring the heart • consecrating to Christ • cultivating the new man • instructing in the knowledge of salvation —*Making conscience the cause* 3. The effect: Freedom through character growth.

©2013 The Foundation for American Christian Education

The Impact of Christ in Education

The end of learning is to repair the ruins of our first parents by regaining to know God aright and out of that knowledge to love Him, to imitate Him, to be like Him. —John Milton, *Of Education*

Christian education should reflect the impact of Christ—a new spirit and a new power in education. Christian education, in and of itself, is not a means of salvation for the individual or the nation, but rather preparation for salvation in the unregenerate child and instruction for those who know Jesus Christ as their personal Savior and Lord. In order to fully comprehend true learning from a Biblical perspective, the basic fallen nature of man and the role of education in building individual and national character must be understood.

Christ: The Cornerstone of Education

Jesus Christ, The Living Word, The Logos —John 1

God's Word establishes Biblical reasoning, gives purpose for studying the subject, and reveals the nature and character of God in the subject. The study of each subject begins with the Word of God. The subject is illuminated through its Biblical principles and the pathway of reasoning is directed toward true understanding. This approach challenges teachers and students to continually research God's Word and primary sources, rather than being dependent upon textbooks, most of which reflect a secular view of education, government, and history.

Jesus Christ, The Focal Point of All History —Ephesians 1:9–10

The Principle Approach® places great emphasis on the providential works of God in history, His Hand in human affairs. God is the sovereign Lord of nations as well as of individuals, having a plan and purpose for each. Principle Approach students, studying the Scriptures and primary sources such as the political sermons of colonial pastors and the writings of our Founding Fathers, discover the primacy of long-neglected Biblical principles in shaping America and the American consciousness.

Every American needs to be re-educated as to God's providence in the founding of our nation and of our unique purpose as the first nation in the history of the world to express the Christian idea of man and government. Our government, laid out in Biblical form in our Constitution, expresses the purposes of establishing civil and religious liberty and a Christian civilization and culture which give glory to God.

Jesus Christ, The Master Teacher —John 3:2

Jesus touched individuals, causing each person to feel especially loved. Teaching is in essence a relationship between the teacher and the student through a subject. To teach Christianly is to examine the Master Teacher and learn from Him. Jesus taught by modeling and is the archetype of teaching, the standard, the ideal. Through His Son, God answered the question of what teaching is. Jesus taught by loving, accepting, affirming, receiving. He taught by healing, by enabling, by prodding. He imparted truth in such a way that its intrinsic beauty delighted his students, captivated their hearts and minds, so much so that two thousand years later, we are touched by His words and respond to His message with our hearts.

The Christian Idea of the Child

And they brought young children to him, that he should touch them: and his disciples rebuked those that brought them. But when Jesus saw it, he was much displeased, and said unto them, Suffer the little children to come unto me, and

©2013 The Foundation for American Christian Education

forbid them not: for of such is the kingdom of God. Verily I say unto you, Whosoever shall not receive the kingdom of God as a little child, he shall not enter therein. And he took them up in his arms, put his hands upon them, and blessed Them.
—Mark 10:13–16

Christian education should see the individual child as possessing an independent value apart from the class group and its agenda. Christianity's central doctrine, that man was created in the Divine image and destined for immortality, pronounces that in the eye of God all children are equal. This shift in view requires a new approach to the classroom, the curriculum, the methodology, and a new role for the teacher of children. Principle Approach® education applies the methods that honor the child's innate value in Christ and lays a foundation of Biblical principle and precept in every subject while forging the character that is Christian—Christ within. This is the Christian idea of the child!

Read the article
"The Christian Idea of the Child,"
by Dr. Carole G. Adams.

(Originally published in the *Journal of F.A.C.E.*, Vol. II, 1990; Revised and republished in *Family and the Nation: Biblical Childhood*, Rosalie J. Slater. F.A.C.E., 2002.

©2013 The Foundation for American Christian Education

Lesson 5

Our Heritage of Christian Education

What's Wrong?	Let's Solve It!
Without principles and "knowledge of the past," we cannot recognize the better way!	Learn to discern true methods and curriculum. Examine Biblical models.

LESSON 5 — ASSIGNMENTS

READINGS

1. Lesson 5
2. Pages 602–616 in *Christian History of the American Revolution: Consider and Ponder*: "The Education of John Quincy Adams."
3. Who were his teachers?
4. What were the texts that were cited? Describe the qualities of his character and scholarship.

REFLECTIONS

Study the CHRISTIAN EDUCATION TIMELINE on p. 49. What is your role as an American Christian educator? Be specific!

WRITING

Apply definitions, principles, and distinctives gleaned from this lesson to your "Educational Philosophy Chart"; layout for photocopying found on pages 98–101.

©2013 The Foundation for American Christian Education

OUR HERITAGE OF CHRISTIAN EDUCATION

Hear, O Israel: The Lord our God is one Lord: And thou shalt love the Lord thy God with all thine heart, and with all thy soul, and with all thy might. And these words, which I command thee this day, shall be in thine heart: And thou shalt teach them diligently unto thy children, and shalt talk of them when thou sittest in thine house, and when thou walkest by the way, and when thou liest down, and when thou risest up.

—Deuteronomy 6:4–7

History of American Christian Education

Essential for every Christian parent and teacher is an understanding of the distinctives of American Christian Education. Each of us, products of twentieth century secular education, has been robbed and pillaged of the knowledge of America's rich Christian heritage.

American Christian Education, the Principle Approach®, has restored America's historic method of Christian education practiced in the founding generations. Like the Christian day and home schools in those eras, it places primary emphasis on learning and applying the Truths of the Bible and principles of the Protestant Reformation upon which American government and education originally were built. It is helpful to know the history of Biblical Christian education and the distinctives that produced such scholar-statesmen as Washington, Jefferson, Franklin, Monroe, Madison, John and Samuel Adams, and Marshall—all of whom were educated in the colonies.

Colonial America's education is Biblical in form and spirit and requires an understanding of God's commands and instructions to Israel, His covenant nation. God sovereignty established His covenant through Abraham, the father of the nation, Israel. Therefore, the precepts of Biblical education are rooted in the overarching mind-set of the Hebrew writers of Scripture.

Contrasting Two Historic Worldviews of Education

	Hebrew Mind-Set	Greek Mind-Set
Education Begins:	Knowledge of God	Knowledge of man
Essential Quality:	Holiness of God	Transference of knowledge
Education for:	All the people	Wealthy and leisure classes
Education to Develop:	The whole person	Aptitudes and talents
Why Learn:	To revere God	To comprehend
Object of Education:	Know God and submit to the authority of His Word	Know thyself

©2013 The Foundation for American Christian Education

The cultural mind-set of Israel, the covenant nation of God, was vastly different from the cultural mind-set of ancient pagan Greek thought and culture. In comparison with other cultures, Jewish education was meant to be education with a difference. Designed to educate the whole person, the essential quality of holiness (the separation from all other peoples and their contaminating pagan philosophies in order to belong to God) established the great contrast between the Greek and the Hebrew worldviews of education—Deuteronomy, chapter six.[1]

Education for the Jew was centered in God and was life-oriented (not centered in man and information-driven). They used the context of daily life to teach God's precepts and statutes in all subjects.

In American education today, the contrast between the Biblical Christian philosophy of education and the progressive secular philosophy is the same. It should be noted, however, that. *most Christian curriculum in America today is rooted in a secular mind-set.* Knowing the history of American education will convince you that each of us must labor to restore God's Word to the heart of teaching and learning. Please take time to study the timeline on page 49.

Three Biblical educators (priest-teachers) are worthy of study: Samuel, Ezra, and Jesus Christ. When their life accounts, their childhood education, the curriculum and methods they used as teachers, and the effect upon the character of their nation are studied together, an educational paradigm emerges—one that found expression in the Protestant Reformation and subsequently in the American colonies.

Old Testament Model: Samuel's Schools of the Prophets

"The child Samuel ministered unto the Lord before Eli. And the word of the Lord was precious in those days; there was no open vision."

—I Samuel 3:1

Samuel, the child dedicated by his mother to education under the nurture of Israel's high priest, Eli, knew firsthand the tragedy of the omission of Godly education in a nation. As a judge, priest, and prophet of Israel, he witnessed its effect in the moral degradation of his people and their national character. His solution was to establish "schools of the prophets" to restore the knowledge of God in all subjects—in the arts, the sciences, in literature, and history. In only twenty years, Samuel's restoration of Biblical education turned his nation back to God and established her character and identity as a God-chosen people—one called to be a light unto the world.

Early trained to love the glorious national traditions of the past, he was a witness of the moral degeneracy of his nation's leaders. The sanctuary, destitute of the ark and tended by a decaying priesthood, had also fallen into utter disregard. In these troublesome days, the Hebrew culture—music, art, and poetry—and its history were unknown. Samuel gathered disciples, or "sons of the prophets," into small "schools" (I Samuel 19:20) at Samaria, Gilgal, Bethel, Ramah, Shiloh, and Jericho to restore both religious and cultural literacy. This free education,[2] which highlighted composition, the study of sacred history and law, and hymnology, was open to all—the herdsman, the potter, the merchant, the farmer. When educated, the prophet would return to his farm or some occupation connected with city life.

Imagine the impact of just one man educated in God's Law, returning to his community to teach others. Not only did these sons of the prophets raise Israel's level of literacy, but they were the great means of maintaining the worship of God among the people. They had been taught the type of life which every member of a covenant nation ought to lead. Ellicott suggests that King

[1] See also *Our Father Abraham: Jewish Roots of The Christian Faith* by Marvin R. Wilson, William B. Eerdmans Publishing Co., Grand Rapids, MI, 1989, pp. 287–291.

[2] *An Old Testament Commentary* edited by Charles John Ellicott, D.D., Cassel & Company, Limited, London, 1887, Vol. II, p. 290.

©2013 The Foundation for American Christian Education

Christian Education Timeline

Eternity Past

Era	Date	Event
Creation		"In the beginning was the Word . . ."
The fall of man Pagan idea of man & government		Reasoning corrupted by deception—the need for a Savior
Moses & the Law	 1450	The Eternal Law God's instructions for education given—Deu. 6
Moral preparation for the Gospel	1100s	Samuel's Schools of the Prophets
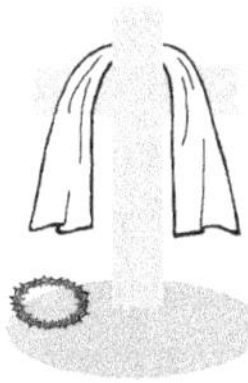	458	Ezra restored God's Word to the heart of education; compiled Old Testament canon
Jesus Christ Focal point of history Christian idea of man & government		Jesus—"The Way, the Truth, and the Life" The *Logos—The* Master Teacher
	33	Pentecost—The Holy Spirit of Truth—"The Teacher sent to abide within the believer."
Paul & the Christian Church	50	The Gospel traveled westward.
Medieval Era	500	Lack of God's Word caused ignorance, fear, & rampant illiteracy.
Bible in English	 1380	Wycliffe—"Morning Star of the Reformation" God's Word available for the individual—revival of the mind inspired new ideas in the arts and sciences
Columbus	 1492	"Christ-bearer" to the New World
The Reformation	1500s	Tyndale, The Great Bible, The Geneva Bible Martin Luther & John Calvin; Biblical education restored. The Bible became "The First Book of instruction."
Christian Founding	 1620	Flowering of English language; Bible became political textbook; Seed of Christian Republic planted Christian colleges founded—God's Word at the heart of education. Colonial education produced highest rate of literacy in world!
American Christian Republic Pastors, Patriots, & Pioneers	 1776	Declaration of Independence—U.S. Constitution Christian civil government founded on God's Law
Expansion & Erosion	 1828	Flowering of America—invention & enterprise Noah Webster, father of American education Horace Mann, father of progressive education
	1900s	John Dewey expounds socialism in education; moral decay, cultural decline; illiteracy
Restoration	 2000	The need for Christians to restore God's Word to the heart of education

______________________________ Your Name

Eternity Future

©2013 The Foundation for American Christian Education

David was a graduate of Samuel's school. The prophetic order, which continued for over eight hundred years was also a permanent public power alongside the priesthood and the office of king—a powerful influence rooted in the divine Word of God. Israel was restored in twenty years through the impact of these graduates of the Schools of the Prophets and slowly rose to a new independent position among pagan nations. The writings of Rosalie Slater suggest the following fruit:[1]

National Poets: extolling the mercies of the Lord and His great goodness to Israel, evidenced in the poetry of Kings David and Solomon and other unidentified psalmists;

Moral Teachers: leading Israel back to the great rock of Mosaic morality, bursting forth into a cleansing stream of individual and national reformation;

Annalists: recounting as historians the providential events in God's blessings to the nation, enabling the Jews to be a "God-remembering people" once again;

Patriotic Preachers: preserving Israel's national identity;

Pastors: shepherding and teaching with the "rod and staff" of the Great Shepherd;

Exponents of the Law: dealing with obedience to the Ten Commandments;

Politicians: preaching the polity of God's jurisdiction and government of man and the universe, and of Israel's direct rule by God.

New Testament Model: Compulsory Education in the Day of Jesus Christ

"And the child grew and waxed strong in spirit, filled with wisdom: and the grace of God was upon him." —Luke 2:40

The child-life of Jesus and His education are briefly stated in the Scriptures, as He passed from infancy to manhood in a tiny Galilean village called Nazareth. However, it is the fruit of thousands of years of the nurturing Hebrew home, distinct from those of the pagan world.

Education for the Jew began in the home, as parents took seriously the role of equipping character through moral teachings. Jewish fathers and mothers had the centuries-old traditions and mores imprinted upon them as modeled by their Heavenly Father. From birth, a religious atmosphere surrounded the child of Jewish parents through the rite of circumcision, when his name was first spoken in prayer and the child henceforth was separated unto God.

A child's first education was the responsibility of the mother. Most likely, the toddler would follow her around as she dispensed her religious household duties: the Sabbath meals, the kindling of the Sabbath lamp, the setting apart of a portion of the dough from the bread for the household, the duty of the mezuza—the symbol of divine guard over the Israelite home. She would sing and tell him the national history and the stories of God's providential hand of protection and guidance. Long before the child went to school or even synagogue, the private and united prayers and domestic rites would indelibly impress themselves upon his mind. Mothers knew the Scriptures and would teach them orally to their young babes.[2]

Jews were from their swaddling clothes trained to recognize God as their Father and Creator of the world. The child bore in the image of his soul God's Law, and was made acquainted with the acts of his predecessors in order to imitate them.

While a child's earliest religious training came from the lips of his mother, it was his father who was bound to teach his son. Soon the child would learn his religious instructions, memorize portions of Scriptures, the Jewish liturgy, short

[1] *The Family and the Nation: Biblical Childhood* by Rosalie J. Slater. Foundation for American Christian Education, 2002, p. 137.

[2] *The Life and Times of Jesus the Messiah* by Alfred Edersheim. Original printing 1886; Hendrickson Publishers, Inc., 1993, pp. 229–230.

©2013 The Foundation for American Christian Education

prayers, and select sayings of the sages. Most Jewish homes had possession of some portion of the Word of God in the original—a most cherished treasure. Special attention was given to the culture of the *memory* since forgetfulness might prove as fatal as ignorance or neglect of God's Law.

Every Jewish child was sent to school for formal primary instruction and training at the age of five or six. Compulsory education existed and in Jerusalem, at the time of Herod, it was deemed unlawful to live in a place where there was no school. From the book of Leviticus—God's instruction in holiness—came the first lessons for every Jewish child. Such were the circumstances and influences of the early years of Jesus of Nazareth. From His intimate familiarity with Holy Scriptures, it can be inferred that his humble home must have surely possessed a precious copy of the Sacred Volume in its entirety.[1] Jesus, "Rabboni—*The* Master Teacher," is our model teacher. His teaching techniques should be studied and applied by every pastor, educator, and parent. A good resource is *Teaching Techniques of Jesus* by Herman Horne, first edition 1920, still available in religious book stores today.

America's Colonial and Founding Model

"The education of our children is never out of my mind. Train them to virtue. Habituate them to industry, activity, and spirit!"

—Letter from John to Abigail Adams, 1777

America has a rich heritage of excellence in education. Its seedbed is the colonial period when the Bible of the Reformation, "the book of all learning," traveled westward to the North American continent. It was a child's first *reader,* or primer, at the knees of his mother, as well as his father's political textbook for after dinner discussions around the fire.

As family, church, and community life were carved out of the wilderness, children were home schooled, taught to read, catechized, and carefully instructed on how to reason from the Word of God for solutions in every sphere of life. Only sixteen years after the arrival of the Pilgrims, Harvard College was established for the purpose of training ministers to preach the Gospel and to teach their congregations how to think and reason Biblically.

Parents took seriously their role of educating their children and of building strong Christian character for future citizenry and leadership. From the pen of John Adams to his wife and "dearest friend":

> "Education makes a greater difference between man and man, than nature has made between man and brute. The virtues and powers to which men may be trained, by early education and constant discipline, are truly sublime and astonishing. . . . It should be your care therefore, and mine, to elevate the minds of our children, and exalt their courage, to accelerate and animate their industry and activity, to excite in them an habitual contempt of meanness, abhorrence of injustice and inhumanity, and an ambition to excel in every capacity; faculty, and virtue. If we suffer their minds to grovel and creep in infancy, they will grovel and creep all their lives." [2]

The emphasis on the Bible as the primer, or first book of learning during America's founding generation, not only produced the highest literacy rate of any period in history,[3] but produced individuals of ennobled Christian character and scholarship, who cherished individual liberty with law and birthed our Christian constitutional republic. The men who wrote America's State Papers were all educated in the colonies. Their testimony has left us a model of Christian education for a Christian civilization.

[1] Edersheim, p. 233.

[2] The *Christian History of the American Revolution: Consider and Ponder* by Verna M. Hall, Foundation for American Christian Education, 1975, p. 606.

[3] *American Education: The Colonial Experience* 1607–1783, by Lawrence A. Cremin, Harper & Row, Publishers, NY, 1970, p. 546.

©2013 The Foundation for American Christian Education

Colonial American Education

"the ordinary road of Hornbook, Primer, Psalter, Testament, and Bible." —John Locke, 1690

The Hornbook:
A flat piece of wood with a handle upon which a sheet of paper was attached and covered with transparent animal horn. It was tied to the young child's waist.

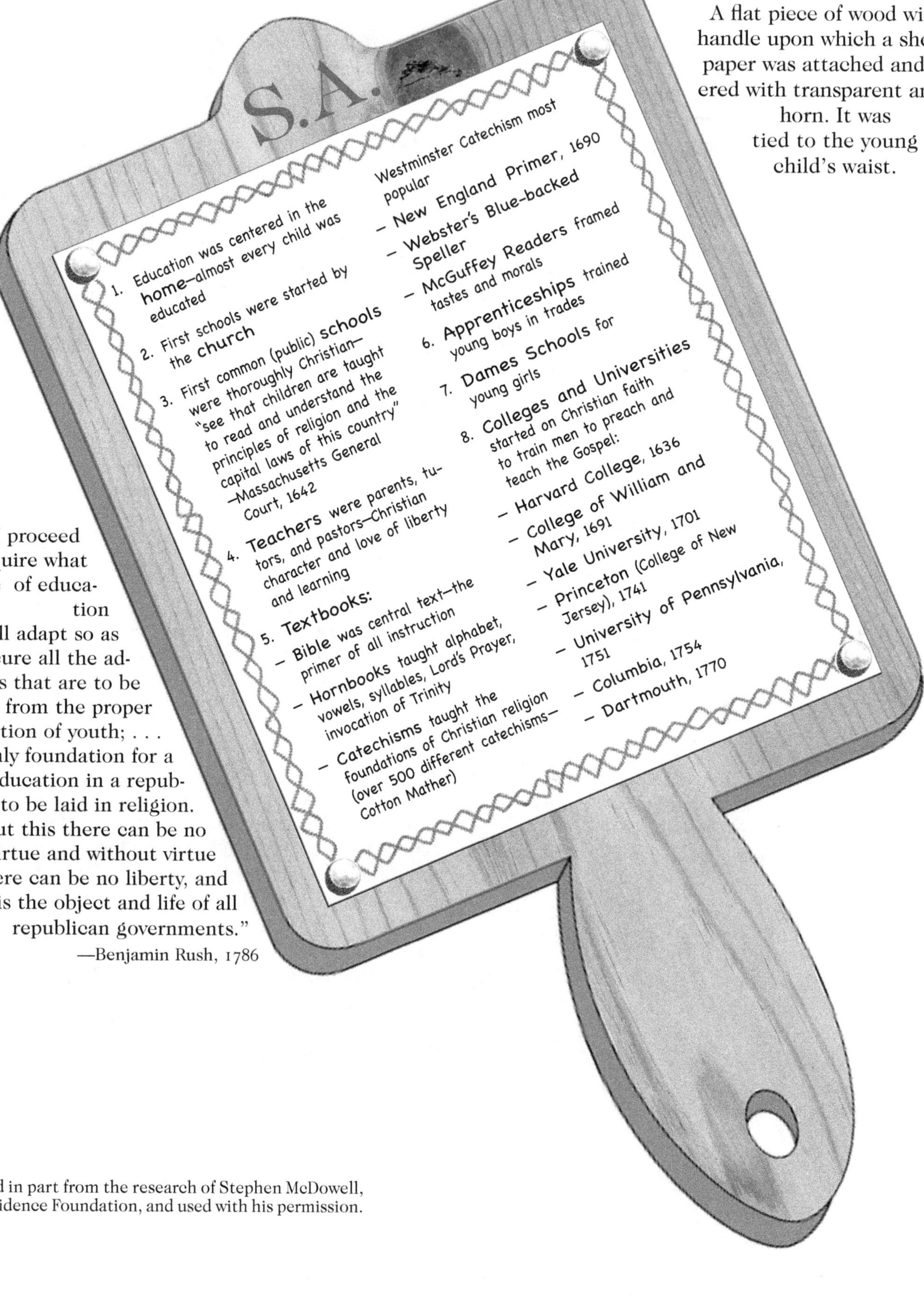

S.A.

1. Education was centered in the **home**—almost every child was educated
2. First schools were started by the **church**
3. First common (public) **schools** were thoroughly Christian—"see that children are taught to read and understand the principles of religion and the capital laws of this country" —Massachusetts General Court, 1642
4. **Teachers** were parents, tutors, and pastors—Christian character and love of liberty and learning
5. **Textbooks:**
   - **Bible** was central text—the primer of all instruction
   - **Hornbooks** taught alphabet, vowels, syllables, Lord's Prayer, invocation of Trinity
   - **Catechisms** taught the foundations of Christian religion (over 500 different catechisms—Cotton Mather) Westminster Catechism most popular
   - **New England Primer**, 1690
   - **Webster's Blue-backed Speller**
   - **McGuffey Readers** framed tastes and morals
6. **Apprenticeships** trained young boys in trades
7. **Dames Schools** for young girls
8. **Colleges and Universities** started on Christian faith to train men to preach and teach the Gospel:
   - **Harvard College**, 1636
   - **College of William and Mary**, 1691
   - **Yale University**, 1701
   - **Princeton** (College of New Jersey), 1741
   - **University of Pennsylvania**, 1751
   - **Columbia**, 1754
   - **Dartmouth**, 1770

"I proceed inquire what mode of education we shall adapt so as to secure all the advantages that are to be derived from the proper instruction of youth; . . . the only foundation for a useful education in a republic is to be laid in religion. Without this there can be no virtue and without virtue there can be no liberty, and liberty is the object and life of all republican governments."
—Benjamin Rush, 1786

Designed in part from the research of Stephen McDowell, The Providence Foundation, and used with his permission.

Summary of Common Educational Distinctives

Samuel's Schools of the Prophets, 1100 B.C.

Jewish Compulsory Schools, Time of Christ

Founding Generations of America, A.D. 1620–1783

1. *Scripture* was at the heart of learning—the primer or first book of instruction—guiding reading lessons, governing thinking, transforming the carnal mind to one of holiness and consecration.

2. Educating the *whole* man was emphasized.

3. Training the faculty of *memory* was of primary importance.

4. Young men were taught to *reason* from the *revelation of God's Work* God's principles illuminated and governed all subjects, directing a pathway of reasoning for life. Years were spent studying logic, the "art of just reasoning."

5. *Languages,* particularly the original languages of the Bible, were taught.

6. *Composition* was central to learning. Youth were required to write out their thoughts and reasoning in an articulate way, guided by the beauty and elevation of the Scriptures, the highest standard of language.

7. Learning and revelation were laboriously *recorded* in copybooks for a permanent record of reflection.

8. *Providential history* was taught from the Word of God and pious models of character were upheld for emulation.

9. *Rhetoric,* "the art of logical expression," was studied, enabling young men to defend their reasoning and worldview publicly.

10. The *fine arts* were emphasized, training the aesthetic tastes of the brute nature of man.

11. The natural *sciences* were studied, as well as philosophy.

12. Young men were equipped with a *virtuous character to govern* themselves privately and publicly with the *sense of duty to serve,* domestically and politically.

America's Educational Decline

Throughout history, liberty in learning is consistently linked with the availability of the Scriptures in the hands of the individual, his ability to read, and his subsequent obedience to study and apply God's principles to his personal and public life.

The holy flame of Scripture in American education has sadly been extinguished over the past one hundred fifty years. The Bible as a first book of knowledge has subtly been removed from the heart of education beginning with Horace Mann's concept of public education in the 1830s. Several generations later, America was to bear the bitter fruit of a national character ripe for socialism.

With the writing of the *Humanist Manifesto I* of the 1930s and John Dewey's establishment of progressive education based on the anti-Christian philosophy of socialism came ignorance, illiteracy, and moral decline in all spheres of American life. Tragically, Scriptural principles were replaced by false theories, God's Hand in America's history and government removed from history texts, and the Biblical meanings of American English words removed from dictionaries. Americans exchanged a Biblical Christian world and life view for a pagan secular worldview.

Restoring America's Heritage of Biblical Education

If the foundations are destroyed, what can the righteous do? —Psalm 11:3

The ability of the Principle Approach® to restore Christian character and scholarship to American education, while teaching our youth God's

©2013 The Foundation for American Christian Education

providential hand in relation to America and her uniquely Christian institutions, is now evidenced in thousands of educators and students around the nation. With its foundation rooted in the Biblical and colonial American models of education, it provides a whole educational program that can be implemented today by Christians around the world.

The requirement for restoring America's heritage of Biblical education is for each Christian educator to commit himself to personal research and study beginning with his own philosophy of education. Will you make that commitment for equipping this next generation of leaders for the twenty-first century?

©2013 The Foundation for American Christian Education

Lesson 6

Gaining a Providential View of History

The Noah Plan®

Biblical • Classical • American Education

What's Wrong?	Let's Solve It!
I'm indoctrinated by a materialistic, hedonistic, "me" and "now" focus. I am not the center of the universe or the sum total of existence.	Get a worldview that is true! Learn *His* story!

Lesson 6 — Assignments

Readings

1. Lesson 6
2. Pages 46–54 in *Christian History of the American Revolution: Consider and Ponder*: "The Hand of God in American History."
3. Pages Ia–XIV, 1–9 in *The Christian History of the Constitution*, Vol. I.
4. Complete the assigned lesson readings in *Teac-hing and Learning America's Christian History: The Principle Approach* by Rosalie Slater for "The Seven Principles of American Christian History and Government" on pp. 63–87.
5. Pages 280–301 in *Teaching and Learning*—a short biography of Noah Webster.
6. There is a biography of Noah Webster on the green pages in Webster's 1828 *Dictionary* and an article about Noah Webster by Stephen McDowell in *The Journal of F.A.C.E.*, Vol. V for you to read.

Reflections

1. Study the Sample *Christian History Study* on Noah Webster on pp. 81–82.
2. Study the Christian Education Timeline, p. 49.
3. What is your role as an American Christian educator?

Writing

1. Complete a Providential History Timeline for yourself.
2. Apply definitions and principles gleaned from this lesson to your "Educational Philosophy Chart"; layout for you to photocopy found on pages 98–101.

©2013 The Foundation for American Christian Education

Gaining a Providential View of History

The hand of our God is upon all them for good that seek him; but his power and his wrath is against all them that forsake him.

— Ezra 8:22

Providence: The Hand of God in History

"In *theology*, the care and superintendence which God exercises over his creatures. He that acknowledges a creation and denies a *providence*, involves himself in a palpable contradiction; for the same power which caused a thing to exist is necessary to continue its existence. Some persons admit a *general providence*, but deny a *particular providence*, not considering that a *general providence* consists of particulars. A belief in divine *providence* is a source of great consolation to good men. By divine *providence* is often understood God himself." —Noah Webster, 1828 *Dictionary.*

The Providence of God in history is a Biblical doctrine. Divine Providence, understood as God Himself, filled the literature of England and Amer-ica for over 500 years until the twentieth century. Abundant evidence can be found in the original historical documents and in the writings of English and American historians. The Principle Approach philosophy of education and government is the Providential view of history. As American Christians, we know something of the saving grace of Christ, but very little about how God brought forth this nation. This ignorance of the Hand of God in America has diluted our love for our nation and our uniquely Christian institutions. If we do not know of God's directing Hand in America's past, how can we be certain of it today or in the future? The consequence of this uncertainty is the lack of knowledge of our own call and purpose in God's plan for us as individuals and the nation at large.

Raised in a secular educational environment, America and Christianity have become separated in our thinking. Identified in an address to the Pilgrim Seminar in Plymouth, Verna M. Hall profiled modern Christians in two categories: One group is "known for attempting to make Christianity more human and more like secular institutions in attempting to solve our national problems. Indeed it is difficult to tell where this type of Christianity leaves off and good humanism begins. The other group has become so concerned with endeavoring to defend the faith itself, that they have withdrawn almost completely from the affairs of man in his daily walk. . . . forgetting or forsaking the Hand of God in history, forgetting or forsaking the Word of God as our American political textbook, our economic textbook, our social, cultural, educational textbook; this alone has produced the results we have in our nation today." *

Providence is the *key* to understanding history as it reveals God's Hand moving in the affairs of individuals and of nations to fulfill His purposes here on earth. It presents the whole view from eternity's perspective. It plants hope and purpose in the hearts and minds of individuals, challenging them to assume their God-ordained purposes in directing human events.

* Verna M. Hall, excerpts from an address to the First Pilgrim Seminar, Plymouth, MA, November 18, 1971.

©2013 The Foundation for American Christian Education

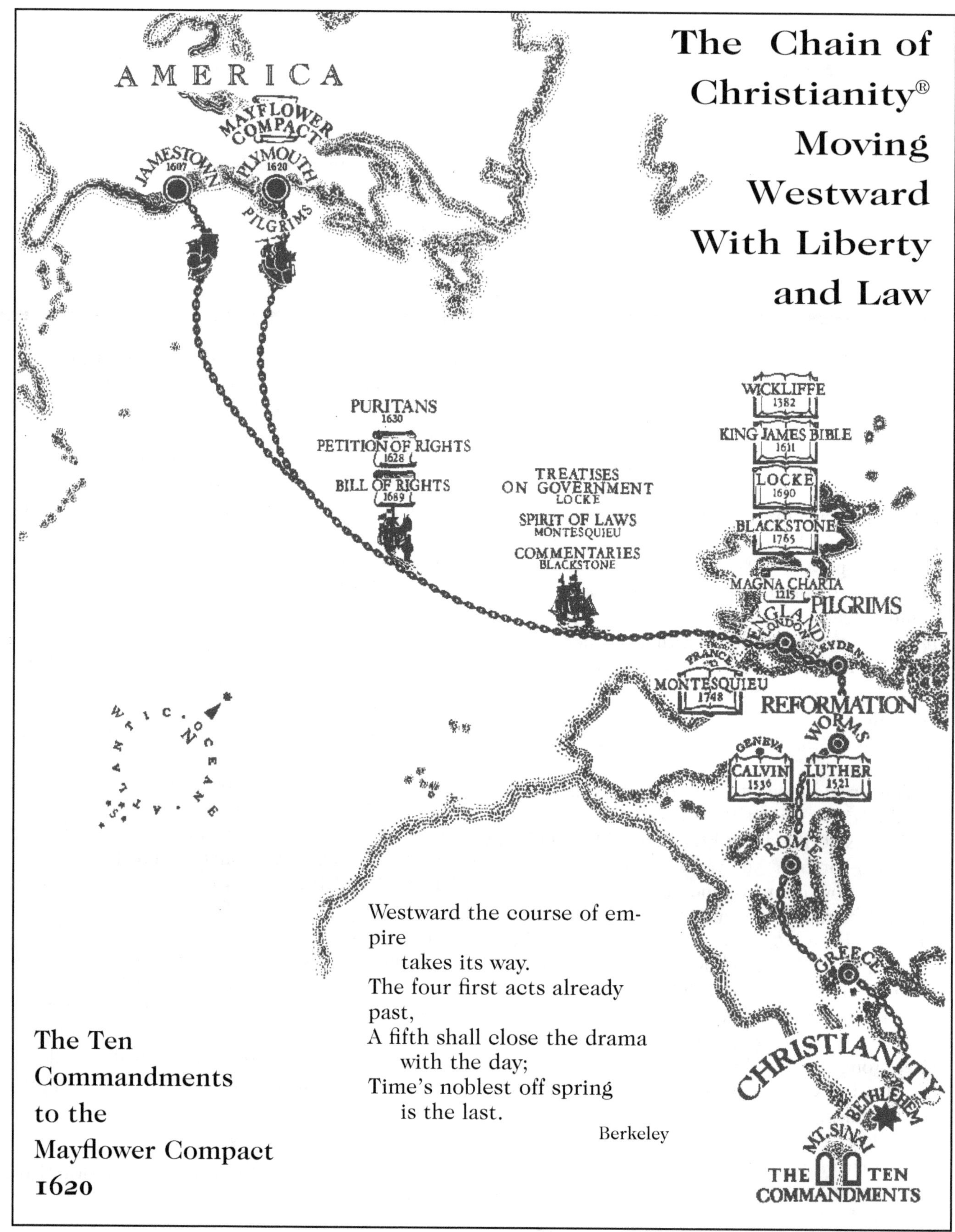

©2013 The Foundation for American Christian Education

Teaching Subjects Providential Answers:

Who? God—His Sovereignty, His Purpose, His Nature, His Character

What? Events and Individuals

Where? Geography—the Stage for Man's Activities

Why? The Gospel Purpose for the Subject

The Chain of Christianity®

The Chain of Christianity is defined as God's use of individual men and of nations to move the Gospel westward and to effect internal liberty in the civil sphere. The concept of the Chain of Chris-tianity has several themes:

1. How are men governed?
2. How did God use individual character to forward Christ, His Story? *

Since Adams's disobedience and fall, man has been trying to establish a government to hold in check his wickedness and inhumanity. While God's principles were related to the civil sphere, the concept of individual liberty came into existence and increased the desire to restrain the power of government over those it governed. It took 1620 years from the time Jesus Christ appeared for Christian liberty to be seen as God-given, not government granted. The Pilgrims understood that government is first *internal* as each individual accepts the liberty which only Christ can give. It is *external* in the civil sphere and, if Christian in nature, will reflect a greater freedom from the restriction of government in the life of the individual. The concept of gov-ernment on the Chain of Christianity reveals more liberty for the individual as the Gospel continues moving westward. Liberty culminated in the civil sphere in America with the formation of the world's first Christian constitutional republic. This is one of two major themes that should be taught to the student every year, beginning in kindergarten.

The second theme that should be included when teaching the Chain of Christianity is how God has used individual character to forward His plan and purposes on the earth. After the appearance of Jesus Christ, the focal point of all history, character became related to individual salvation. The Old Covenant required obedience to God's Law which was written on stone tablets. However, in the New Covenant, God's indwelling Spirit writes His Law on the tablets of human hearts and minds, providing greater internal liberty.

A timeline is an excellent tool for illustrating the major links on the Chain of Christianity. One should be developed for each classroom and hung over the chalkboard for easy reference and use in all subjects. See an example of a timeline on page 45 and a discussion of timelines with an example on the following pages.

Key Links on America's Christian History Timeline

"For God has allowed us to know the secret of his plan, and it is this: He purposed long ago in his sovereign will that all human history should be consummated in Christ."

—Ephesians 1:9–10 (Phillips)

History is "Christ, *His* Story." As Christians we recognize that God is the disposer of men and nations for His purposes and plans and ultimately for His glory. In His sovereignty, God assigned to each nation a special role to play, contributions to make, and all of these *separate stones* and *pillars* became building blocks to be used by *the Master Builder* as the Chain of Christianity moved westward to America.

The Christian history timeline for primary and elementary grades contains ten key links from

* *Rudiments of America's Christian History and Government: Student Handbook* by Rosalie J. Slater and Verna M. Hall, F.A.C.E., 1968, revised second edition 1994, pp. 45–83.

©2013 The Foundation for American Christian Education

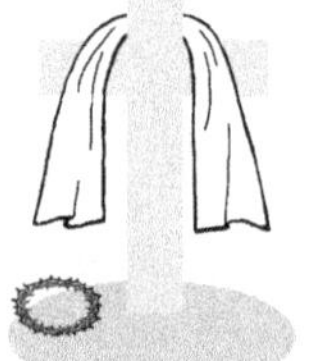

Creation	Moses and The Law	Jesus Christ, the Focal Point of History	Paul & the Christian Church	The Bible in English
	1450		50	1380

the Chain of Christianity. These same ten links are found on each timeline developed, regardless of the subject, individual, event, or nation researched and presented. They are the key individuals, key leading ideas, key nations, or key events that God, in His sovereign Providence, purposes for Christ, His Story in the westward course of the Law and Gospel. These major links illustrate and teach the two themes of the Chain of Christianity.

God created and fashioned everything for His purpose. Therefore, every subject has a Biblical foundation, every subject has a Christian history, every subject has a Gospel purpose! When teachers identify and organize their curriculum in this manner, every teacher becomes a Christian history teacher. This method of curriculum developed and classroom presentation shifts the emphasis in teaching and learning from memorizing and parroting information and facts to thinking and reasoning from leading ideas and principles. This shift in curriculum development and teaching methods firmly establishes the Biblical principles upon which students can interpret the cause and effect of all historic and current events.

The same ten key links on the Chain of Christianity are presented chronologically each year in the elementary history curriculum, beginning with "Creation" and ending with "Restoration." A different link is highlighted and taught in depth each year. The seedbed of each link—is presented in the kindergarten—the primary, recurring Biblical principles and leading ideas—is presented in the kindergarten program and expanded throughout the years. Following is a brief overview of each major link developed from the *Rudiments of America's Christian History and Government* course written by Rosalie J. Slater and Verna M. Hall, 1968 and published by the Foundation for American Christian Education.

The First Link: Creation

God's Principle of Individuality, the key to the study of history, is emphasized and expanded throughout the years to include: God as Creator and Sovereign Ruler; the attributes of God's character and nature; geographic individuals; man is God's property and made in His image; conscience; the fall of man and the need for a Savior; the origin of the races, religions, languages, civilizations; the establishment of civil government.

The Second Link: Moses and the Law

The Providential purpose, preservation, and preparation of Moses, the first historian and lawgiver, are emphasized including: the Ten Commandments—God's eternal Law written on stony tablets; distinctives of moral, ritual, and civil laws; Egypt—a place of refuge; Israel—Hebrew republic; Greece and Rome—pagan republics—aesthetic and political links of preparation for Christianity.

The Third Link: Jesus Christ, the Focal Point of History

In God's fulness of time, He sent His Son to the earth. Christ's birth, death, and resurrection and His eternal effect on history are studied including: Christ's character; Christ fulfilled the Law; God's Law now "written upon fleshly tablets of the heart,"

©2013 The Foundation for American Christian Education

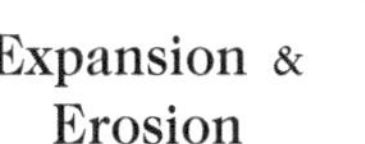

Columbus	Christian Founding	American Christian Republic	Expansion & Erosion	Restoration "*Me*"
1492	**1620**	**1776**	**1800s**	**2000**

the basis for Christian self-government; the Law and the Gospel—the two legs of civil government; the contrast of Christianity and paganism.

The Fourth Link: Paul & the Christian Church

The Apostle Paul, New Testament scholar, heeded the Macedonian cry for help and established the Gospel and the New Testament Church in Europe, turning the course of Christianity westward. The study of this link includes: Paul's missionary journeys; his epistles to the first century Christians and his teachings on civil government; the writing of the New Testament and the establishment of the New Testament Church—a mini-republic.

The Fifth Link: The Bible in English

In order to understand the history of civil liberty, the history of the Bible in English must be studied. Liberty for the individual is directly proportionate to the individual's possession and ability to read the Holy Bible in his own language. Supporting this leading idea is: the *Magna Charta*; how the Bible in the hands of the individual gives rise to an internal reformation and then reformation in the civil sphere: the European Reformation, its reformers and Bible translators—Wycliffe, the "morning star of the Reformation," Tyndale, Coverdale, the Geneva translation, and the King James Authorized Version.

The Sixth Link: Columbus, "Christbearer" to the New World

The preparation of Christopher Columbus, who knew God had a distinct call upon his life, is studied. Providential preparation is evidenced in Marco Polo's journals, Prince Henry's School of Navigation, the invention of navigational instruments and the development of the caravel as the Era of New World Exploration began. One of the themes studied is the preservation of the mainland of North America until God had a people prepared to establish the fullest expression of a Christian civilization.

The Seventh Link: Christian Founding

The Pilgrims and their Christian character became the seed of our American Christian republic. Providentially prepared, the Pilgrims possessed the Christian character, self-government, economics, education, and unity needed to produce a Christian constitutional republic. America's heritage of Christian character, the Providence of God through the Reformation; Holland as a place of refuge; the writing of the *Mayflower Compact*; God's preservation through Squanto; Thanksgiving; fifty-year peace with the Indians; communism versus free enterprise; Bradford's *Of Plimoth Plantation;* and the founding of Jamestown are included.

The Eighth Link: American Christian Republic

As Christianity moved westward with its fullest expression in government, the Christian character of the patriots and pastors of the founding and constitutional eras of our nation and their documents of liberty and contributions are studied: Sam Adams, father of the American Revolution, and his Committees of Correspondence; George Washington, father of our country; Thomas Jefferson; John and Abigail Adams; Benjamin Franklin; Patrick Henry; John

©2013 The Foundation for American Christian Education

Witherspoon; James Madison; John Marshall; the writing of the *Declaration of Independence* and the *U.S. Constitution*.

The Ninth Link: Westward Expansion & Erosion

The Bible, Biblical principles of self- and civil government, and Noah Webster's "Blue-Backed Speller" all went westward with the pioneers and pathfinders. As the nation "flowered," the Era of Enterprise and Invention is highlighted. Other topics covered are: westward expansion; the Civil War; erosion of unity; reconstruction. The character and contributions of such Christian men as Noah Webster, Matthew Maury, Abraham Lincoln, and Robert E. Lee are identified.

The Tenth Link: Restoration, My Place in God's Providence

The role of the American Christian for the twenty-first century is to aid in restoring and reclaiming our heritage of Christian character and civil liberty. God has a unique and special purpose and place on the Chain of Christianity® for each one of us, as well as for each individual nation. Every student is inspired and encouraged to assume his responsibility for the stewardship of his internal and external property, his scholarship and productivity, and to follow Christ in his daily walk, thereby fulfilling God's divine purpose for his life as a young American Christian statesman.

Using a Timeline in Teaching Providential History

The use of a timeline and its role in teaching any subject, especially history, are vital. All subjects have a history and a God-given purpose and should be initially introduced to students by imparting that knowledge. In history there is a natural order, that of chronological sequence. If you mentally examine your own history memory bank, you will find that your understanding of chronology was added piecemeal, as your knowledge of history increased, forming association with prominent events and historic characters. Memorizing a list of dates and events serves no purpose in historic literacy needed to distinguish between the important and the inconsequential. It is of far more value to know the order of the relative significance providentially and to be able to reason from cause to effect. This is where the role of time mapping or the use of a timeline is so worthy.

We are not born with an innate or developed sense of chronology. Time is a developing concept in the young elementary-aged child, one that must be learned. Young children initially require concrete or visual impressions for learning (pictures, maps, globes, handling objects). The abstract capability of reading with symbols must be learned and developed. In order to introduce the concepts of sequence and time, the timeline serves as a concrete method. Children first learn the idea of sequence as a preliminary step for the understanding of chronology and dates later on.

There are many ways to divide time. All of history can be divided into millennia, centuries, or epochs and the critical events and characters mapped that way. But there would be many events that would be inconsequential in the study of the Providential hand of God in history. As the Chain of Liberty moved westward from Creation to the present, ten major events, characters, or links on the Chain of Christianity have been selected. The birth, death, and resurrection of Jesus Christ is the focal point of all history and should be highlighted in some way on each timeline. These links become "pockets" into which children deposit their growing knowledge of history. For example, when the establishment of Jamestown, the first permanent English colony in America, is studied, the children are taught that its founding lies within the same time frame as the American Founding, a major link in America's Christian history. Therefore, children quickly learn the significance of events in God's timetable and then grow in their sense of time and chronology in relation to Christ, His Story.

©2013 The Foundation for American Christian Education

At StoneBridge School, a F.A.C.E. demonstration school in the Principle Approach®, every teacher makes a timeline that is placed over the chalkboard in front of the classroom. Each one reflects the creativity of its designer, but all have the same ten links or "memory pockets" represented. In this way, characters and events that are taught in each grade can be added to highlight the curriculum.

Following are several examples of successful StoneBridge timelines. In kindergarten one teacher used pictures, the same ones she had the student place in their history notebook when they were studied. These pictures represented the event or character of the ten links. She then joined them together with a paper chain. She collected from parents a picture of each of her students and placed them under the tenth link, so that when the children arrived the first day of school, they realized there was something important about the chain on the wall and it had something to do with them!

One sixth grade teacher designed her timeline and placed it on the wall prior to the first day of school. Then in the first few weeks she had the art teacher work with the children to create the figures and representations of event, using construction paper in three-dimensional designs. This was a very successful way of deepening the students' understanding of the value of the timeline and their sense of time and chronology.

A teacher had her six-year-olds create a personal timeline with the help of their parents. Several timelines that were brought in extended nearly the length of the classroom wall! These young children and their parents were drawn into the concepts of the Providential hand of God, sequencing, and time.

Quite often in individual lessons, teachers have asked children to represent characters on the timeline. A human timeline is formed in front of the class and then the character or event being taught that day is represented by a student and placed in the line.

Timelines can be designed vertically or horizontally, and one should always be placed in each student's notebook accompanying the subject overview. When introducing new material, it is very beneficial to have the students quickly draw a timeline in their notes with the ten key links and place the character or event being studied on the timeline in a different color. Then through the years of elementary education, students master the chronology of the Chain of Liberty and are able to place all other historic information within those "memory pockets," discerning whether they contributed to or hindered the westward move of the Gospel. God's plan for internal and external liberty is visually and permanently recorded in their brain!

The Seven Principles of American Christian History and Government

In *Teaching and Learning America's Christian History: The Principle Approach®*, seven principles are identified and defined across the curriculum for the use of educators. These seven principles form the Biblical reasoning in every subject for the teacher and learner. A brief summary and reading guide follows:

I. God's Principle of Individuality:

Everything in God's universe reveals His infinity and diversity. Each person is a unique creation of God, designed to express the nature of Christ individually in society. The parent and teacher cultivate the development and flowering of the talents which God has placed within each child. Do we each appreciate how unique and special each of us is? See *Teaching and Learning*, pp. 65, 141–183.

II. The Christian Principle of Self-Government:

Simply stated, the Christian principle of self-government is God ruling internally from the heart of the individual. In order to have true lib-

©2013 The Foundation for American Christian Education

erty, man must be governed internally by the Spirit of God rather than by external forces. Government is first individual, then extends to the home, church, and the community.

What can self-government mean in the classroom or home school setting? It does not mean relinquishing control to our children. Children need to know the demands upon each one of us and they need to learn how to live with these demands voluntarily. When there is evidence that an individual can begin to assume more responsibility and become "self-governed-under-God" in a few things, then there will be opportunity for more experience. Fortunately, God has provided parents, adults, and teachers to help boys and girls learn how to make choices and decisions which are responsible. There may be mistakes, but if the lesson is pointed out, then Christian self-government has been strengthened. See *Teaching and Learning,* pp. 69–72; 184–209.

III. America's Heritage of Christian Character:

The image of God engraved upon the individual within, brings dominion and change to his external environment. The model of American Christian character is the Pilgrim character, which demonstrates these qualities: *faith and steadfastness, brotherly love, Christian care, diligence and industry, and liberty of conscience.* Learning work habits begins at home and extends into the classroom. Becoming accountable for one's learning and productivity is the fruit of Christian character. See *Teaching and Learning*, pp. 73–75; 210–224.

IV. "Conscience Is the Most Sacred of All Property." (James Madison):

God requires faithful stewardship of all His gifts, especially the internal property of conscience. This is a tool for self-government as each child learns the revelation of consent. Each individual governs his life through the voluntary consent to do right or wrong.

It means to value your Christian conviction and conscience above all external possessions, even life itself, as did the first century Christian martyrs. We learn from our founding fathers that property begins with individual responsibility and productivity —stewardship first, then ownership.

In the home or school setting, property is learned as both internal and external. Not only convictions, but also possessions need to be protected and safeguarded. Property is an individual responsibility and an individual stewardship. Only as it is learned individually will it be mutually valued. How much can you teach of this important principle at home and in the classroom? See *Teaching and Learning,* pp. 65, 141–183.

V. The Christian Form of Our Government:

The divine flow of spiritual power and force through self-governing individuals, whose God-given rights are protected by laws established by their elected representatives. Proper government requires a balance of internal power and its external form as seen in the separation of powers and its dual form with checks and balances. The Christian form of our government finds its source in "the American political textbook"—the Holy Bible, and its principles embody both the law and the Gospel. To make Christian constitutional government effective, the power of government—sovereignty—must be restored to the individual. How important then, to accustom our young children to think of the importance of individual action and influence. See *Teaching and Learning,* pp. 79–81; 240–249.

VI. How the Seed of Local Self-Government Is Planted:

Christian self-government begins with salvation and education in God's Law and Love, and flows in governing oneself, one's home, church, and community. The Chain of Christianity® is made up of individual links. The "mass mind" and the "common man" are empty words; for collectivism

©2013 The Foundation for American Christian Education

is defeated when each individual learns to see himself as God sees him. Even in the family group or the classroom, individuals must take responsibility or blame, in order to discover and correct errors. "Liberty is an individual responsibility." (Sam Adams, Father of the American Revolution.) See *Teaching and Learning* pp. 83–84, 250–261.

VII. The Christian Principle of American Political Union:

Internal agreement or unity, which is invisible, produces an external union, which is visible in the spheres of government, economics, and home and community life. Before two or more individuals can act effectively together, they must first be united in spirit in their purposes and convictions.

The entire program of teaching and learning America's Christian history and form of government is to encourage families and schools to teach with a positive emphasis upon what is right, true, and changeless. The purpose is to provide young people with a dearly defined American Christian standard of reference for every situation. This is "built-in" Christian self-government predicated upon the Word of God. This enables you to extend your influence and example into the lives of our children when we are not with them to guide and counsel.

Educators are encouraged to take the time to clearly define foundations—Christian principles which changelessly turn to the compass point regardless of which direction the individual faces. This will demand of you the vision which keeps you making the sacrifice of time and more time, to think through the lessons which you will teach, and the principles which you must define and redefine by many illustrations and personal example. See *Teaching and Learning,* pp. 85–87; 262–268.

©2013 The Foundation for American Christian Education

Lesson 7

The Curriculum and The Method

The Noah Plan®
Biblical · Classical · American Education

What's Wrong?	Let's Solve It!
Force-fed, worn out, stimulus-response, sensation-injected curricula form the consumer-driven education of today and the resulting dependent character.	Breathe life into learning by daring to research, reason, relate, and record. Cultivate the love of learning!

LESSON 7 — ASSIGNMENTS

READINGS

Pages 102–112, *Teaching and Learning America's Christian History*

REFLECTIONS

Study the methods identified as Biblical. How will they affect your teaching and design of curriculum? This is a very important part of your educational philosophy, for if your methods are not Biblical, they will undermine everything else you attempt.

WRITING

Apply definitions, principles, and distinctives gleaned from this lesson to your "Educational Philosophy Chart"; layout for photocopying found on pages 98–101.

As you begin to develop curriculum for your students, remember to begin with the whole "running course."

©2013 The Foundation for American Christian Education

The Curriculum and the Method

Rigorous teachers seized my youth,
And purged its faith and trimmed its fire,
Showed me the high, white star of Truth,
There bade me gaze and there aspire.
—Matthew Arnold

Education, by definition, is an internal experience. It deals with the eternal nature of man—the spirit, mind, temperament, and character of both teacher and student.

A Christian curriculum should be more than a survival course while waiting for heaven. It should fully equip and train our youth to faithfully serve Christ in their calling as virtuous leaders in every sphere of life. This requires the consistent habit of thinking and reasoning from truth to firmly establish daily spiritual, intellectual, social, and aesthetic sensibilities and disciplines for a Christian world and life view.

Teaching and learning is a natural process and relational—the heart and mind of the teacher interacting with the heart and mind of the student.

Christian education requires a *living* curriculum that *inspires* and *nourishes* the inner man, one rooted in Divine revelation.

What is a *Living* Curriculum?

There is a spirit in man: and the inspiration of the Almighty giveth them understanding. —Job 32:8

Living: *ppr.*, Having life or the vital functions in operation; not dead. 2) Flowing, as a living spring or fountain; not stagnant. 3) Producing action, animation, and vigor; quickening; as a *living* principle; a *living* faith. (Webster's 1828 *Dictionary*)

Curriculum: *n.*, (L. *curriculum*—a running course, race, career.) A specific course of study or, collectively, all the *courses* of study in a school, university, etc.

Course: *n.*, A methodical series, *applied to the arts or the sciences;* a systematized order of princi-ples in arts or sciences, for illustration or instruction.
2) Manner of proceeding; way of life or conduct; deportment; series of actions. *That I might finish my course with joy. Acts xx.* (Webster's 1828 *Dictionary*)

A *curriculum* is:

1. The whole body of knowledge taught—*subjects*
2. How it is ordered—*scope and sequence*
3. The means for teaching it—*methods and tools*

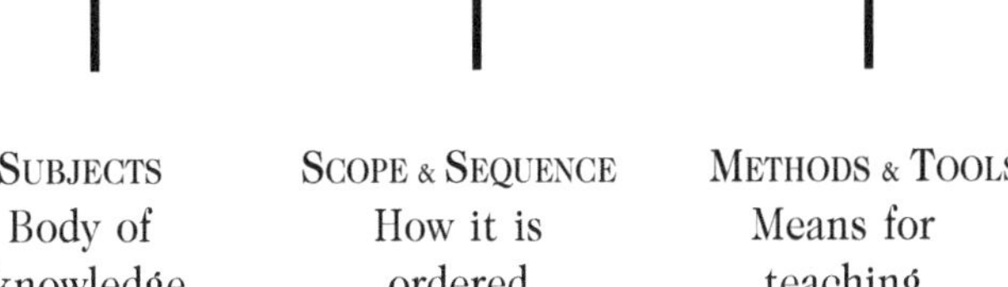

Subjects	Scope & Sequence	Methods & Tools
Body of knowledge taught	How it is ordered	Means for teaching

The goal: To cause effective growth in understanding and character.

©2013 The Foundation for American Christian Education

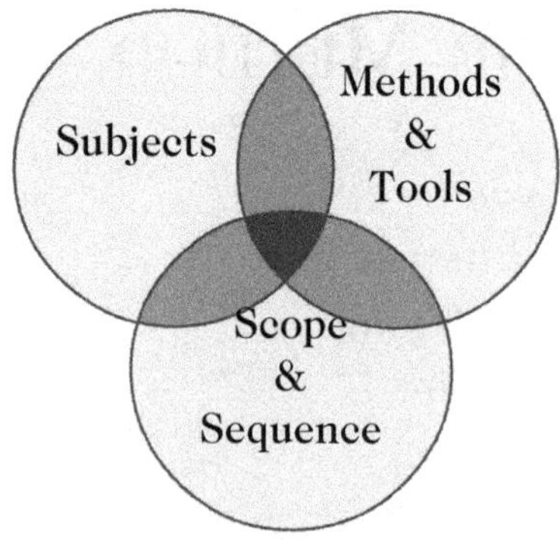

Synergistic:
Each component is interdependent upon the other.

Each component within the curriculum paradigm is ***interdependent*** upon the other. The power of the curriculum resides in both the *internal principles* (educational philosophy) and the *exchange* (synergy) of the components.

To have a living curriculum, each component must be carefully *reasoned*, *ordered*, and *executed* in light of each of the other components in the paradigm. By way of illustration, reason through what the end product of an educational program would be if:

- The subjects do not glorify God and His principles?
- The textbooks are written from a secular worldview?
- The teacher developing the curriculum is not a Christian?
- Secular methods and tools are employed?

The end product would not be Christian education.

Principle Approach® education produces a *living curriculum* because the Truths and authority of God's Word are at the heart of every subject and method. In the Principle Approach, *subjects are unified Biblically, historically, and governmentally.*

The Principle Approach educational program, *The Noah Plan*, is not dependent upon secular textbooks, student workbooks, and teacher manuals with daily lessons fully designed. It *does* provide a scope and sequence, subject guidelines, course overviews, directed courses of study, and Christian methods for teaching and learning, all of which are fully imparted in the F.A.C.E. subject *Curriculum Guides* and the grade-level *Lessons* books. It is a curriculum that is Biblical, historic, and classic by design.

Teaching Methodology Demonstrated in the Bible:

The Bible, given by God to teach man truth, has a unique methodology of teaching which can be characterized as follows:

1. The recurrence of underlying bedrock *principles* forming a unity of truth.
2. The use of *Providential history* to teach the love and character of God.
3. The use of *individual character* to teach the Christian idea of man and government through:
   - The *Notebook Approach*, which governs the teacher and student participation in the subject by establishing a consistent tool and standard of Christian scholarship.
   - The *Four R's*, which form the basic steps of human learning—**research—reason—relate—record.**
   - *Writing overviews* to create a whole approach unified by principles and structure.
   - Emphasis in method on *student participation*, response, essay, discussion, presentation, and the three powers of government—planning, doing, and evaluating.
   - Respect for the individuality of the student through a *tutorial* practice of identification, individualization, record-keeping, in a spirit of love and acceptance believing the best in love, calling forth the full potential of Christ in every child.

©2013 The Foundation for American Christian Education

4. The use of ***stories*** to teach truth the apperception (using the familiar to teach the unfamiliar "living water").
5. The ***wisdom*** of God demonstrated in precepts and principles.
6. The use of ***reasoning with leading ideas and principles*** to teach the "art of learning."
7. The presentation of subject content and principles through the ***life and character of individuals***.
8. The presentation of ***truth in a literary form*** and Biblical standard of language.
9. The use of symbols and imagery, ceremony and celebration to ***memorialize truth***.

See also
"Designing Curriculum Using the Four R's"
Part II, page 110.

The Teacher's Role in American Christian Education

1. Relate to each child individually, calling forth and thereby liberating his individuality in Christ.
2. Inspire a lifelong love of learning, wisdom, and knowledge.
3. Demonstrate the tools of scholarship.
4. Exemplify Christian self-government.
5. Instill the ability to think governmentally.

©2013 The Foundation for American Christian Education

Principled Methodology and Its Results

Whom shall he teach knowledge? And whom shall he make to understand doctrine?
For precept must be upon precept, precept upon precept;
line upon line, line upon line, here a little, and there a little.
—Isaiah 28:9,10

Teachers should accommodate themselves to the capacity of the learners,
give them what they most need, and can best bear, and a little at a time . . .
a variety of instructions [that] might be pleasing and inviting.
—Matthew Henry's Commentary on Isaiah 28:9,10

1. The Bible presents its own unique methodology of teaching.

Practice

- Recurring principles form a unity of truth.
- Leading ideas spring from the principles.
- Providential history teaches the hand of God.
- Subjects presented through the life and character of individuals.
- Liberal use of stories to teach by apperception (ex. living water).
- Upholding a high literary form and style.
- Using symbols, imagery, ceremonies, and celebration to memorialize truth.

[See Herman Harrell Horne, *Teaching Techniques of Jesus,* Kregel Publishing, 1920]

Results

- A divine structure of truth is formed in the student upon which all truth fits in perfect unity.
- Trust in God and faith in His character is inspired.
- A knowledge of man and his human tendencies and inclinations (sin nature) is gained.
- The mind is trained to embrace analogy, to make application of truth.
- Literacy is enhanced and a high standard of language imparted.
- The love of learning is sparked.

2. Reason from the internal to the external, cause to effect.

Practice

- The teacher inspires, consecrates, cultivates, and instructs, and does not stimulate, motivate, enculturate, indoctrinate.

Results

- The student responds to inspiration, consenting to learn and receiving instruction; it is sweet to him.
- Learning is an internal experience informing the heart, appealing to conscience, and affecting the character.

3. Reflective learning and reasoning from principles and leading ideas

Practice

- The pace set by the teacher and the tone of the classroom encourages reflection.
- Questions direct students to identify the causes, the purposes, the underlying truth, the patterns, the problems and solutions.
- Writing is a daily practice in essay, composition, recording discussions, etc.
- Rote learning is used sparingly and only to achieve certain skills.
- Memorization is used to store a bank of meaningful data—poetry, scripture, etc.

Results

- Students are comforted by a sense of importance in what they are learning, and not deadened by busy work.
- Reasoning is the habit of the classroom.
- The student learns to write his thoughts and to articulate the subject.
- Mastery is achieved when the principles are understood and applied, and problems solved by reasoning.
- The student recognizes that his study majors on the majors and prepares him for lifelong learning.

4. The notebook method: three-ring binders with dividers for the organization of the study of the subject

Practice

- The student organizes, according to teacher direction, a notebook for each subject, which he will compile in his own hand.
- It records the research, reason, relating and recording achieved in his study of the subject.
- The standard requires neatness, completeness, accuracy, and order.
- It encourages creativity and individual expression.
- The notebook standard governs the child's study and provides accountability that is personal and particular to each child.

Results

- The notebook habit is teacher-directed in kindergarten and student-generated by middle school building sound study skills and habits.
- It makes the child the producer of his own education.
- It establishes a pace that is reflective allowing successful reasoning through writing, illustration, and articulation.
- It forms Christian character in the student by consistently practicing the standards such as faithfulness, accountability, responsibility, stewardship, thoroughness, work ethic, etc.

5. Essay writing

Practice

- The student learns to invent or combine ideas, clothe them with words, put them in order, and commit them to paper.
- The student is caused to articulate the subject in his own language by writing and presenting.
- Essay writing encourages exact and logical expression of ideas.

Results

- Writing causes clear thinking and careful reasoning.
- The student possesses and masters the subject.
- The student is comfortable with rhetoric and obtains the skills to express himself articulately.

6. Presentation

Practice

- The child presents his own understanding of the lesson or the subject.
- The child exhibits his mastery of the subject through discussion, debate, recitation, presenting his written work, and sharing his reflections and ideas.
- The product of learning is celebrated.

Results

- The child learns to see each individual's expression of the subject as unique and valuable.
- The child values learning as his possession, personal to him, and something to be shared.

7. Tutorial Approach

Practice

- Each child's learning style and pace is valued and honored.
- The child is met at his threshold of learning and taken as far as he can go.
- Teaching isn't complete until learning is achieved.
- Enrichment and remediation are standard practices as needs are recognized.
- The teacher teaches children, not subjects or classes; the individual is valued above the group.

Results

- The student is comfortable with his gifts and confident to rise to challenges.
- Real achievement and excellence are unique to the individual not dependent on the class norm.
- There is no standard rate of learning, style of learning, or "assembly-line" method of learning.
- Teaching is a relationship unique to the individual, based upon respect.
- The love of learning is natural and right.

8. Individual expression through fine and performing arts

Practice

- Children are early introduced to all areas of the arts and given experiences and instructions in all the visual arts, drama, music, dance.
- The arts are integral parts of the learning of every subject in the curriculum.
- Individual expression of the arts is valued and affirmed in all subjects as appropriate and relevant.

Results

- The soul as well as the mind is cultivated and tastes are formed for what is excellent.
- Beauty is a moral teacher: filling the soul with beauty leaves little room for the profane, the mediocre, or the banal.
- Students find expression of talent and ability through the arts and learn to share them to bless others.

9. Word Studies—developing the vocabulary of liberty

Practice

- Word Study as a tool of Biblical scholarship establishes reflective thinking, deductive reasoning, and illumination of the understanding.
- The Word Study builds vocabulary, particularly one of liberty and Biblical government.

Results

- The Word Study builds vocabulary, particularly one of liberty and Biblical government.
- It enhances reading comprehension and verbal scores.

- Practicing the word study with the Webster 1828 *Dictionary* and with the Bible establishes a Biblical vocabulary and precision in the use of words.
- Researching, reasoning, relating, and recording are the four steps of mastery learning.
- Reasoning from cause to effect, from choices to consequences, forms a Biblical world and life view.

- It establishes the precise word usage in writing and oral communication.
- It cultivates the habit of critical thinking.
- It produces deductive reasoning skills.
- It sharpens discernment of truth from error.
- It inculcates a lifetime habit of scholarship.

---

10. Emulation of individual character

Practice

- Teach individual character by introducing individuals who were significant in every subject.
- Teach conscience and character, not circumstances and environment, as causative.
- The study of individuals should include the providential background, the forces of character formation in the life, and the contributions of the individual.

Results

- The student becomes discerning of character qualities that both bless and curse.
- The student becomes acquainted with individuals—forming "friendships"—that will walk with him through life.
- The student discovers role models to emulate in all subjects, giving him the opportunity to identify his own providential calling.

---

11. Overviewing/timelines

Practice

- The subject or lesson is first presented in overview—an outline of what is to be studied.
- The student is encouraged to grasp the scope of his study, the purpose, the outcome.
- The student is shown the subject as a whole, not as a series of lessons that become unrelated over time—but as a whole system of knowledge.

Results

- The student gains a sense of ownership and personal need and responsibility for the subject.
- The student acquires a sense of dominion over the subject.
- The student develops a sense of purpose understanding why the subject is important to him and how it fits into his education.

---

12. Celebration

Practice

- The teacher establishes many celebration opportunities for enjoying what has been learned.
- The teacher enlists help in expanding the student's experiences in the subject—community events, guest scholars, etc.
- Special Days are dedicated to exploring and "handling" the subject.

Results

- Celebration becomes a practice of life, in conformance with Biblical practice.
- The student has opportunity to enjoy learning in various settings and to celebrate his knowledge communally.
- Learning is a joy and fulfills the student's greater need to express his love of God.

The Noah Plan® Curriculum

The scope of *The Noah Plan* Curriculum in Principle Approach® Schools includes language mastery through the study of literature classics, French, Latin, grammar, composition, and research skills. Reasoning skills are developed by studying Bible principles, logic, mathematics, and the sciences. Through the study of history, geography, music and art, students are exposed to a Biblical worldview at the elementary level of education. The mastery of basic skills and habits of scholarship are established in the foundational years, as students are equipped with confidence for success to meet the challenges of a rigorous and demanding high school course of study.

The Noah Plan high school curriculum, developed by masters of subjects, prepares students with the rich vocabulary, reasoning and research skills, and mathematical concepts to compete with high PSAT and SAT (Scholastic Aptitude Test) scores with students from around the nation, enabling their admission to prestigious, conservative colleges and universities with scholarship awards. Armed with a conservative, Biblical world and life view, they place high among their Christian peers as leaders in their own generation. (Please see the PEERS Test results for Principle Approach Schools on page 97.)

Modern and classical languages in high school include four years of French and Spanish, and two years of New Testament Greek. Formal and informal Logic is taught in a demanding Bible curriculum, establishing cogent thinking and Biblical reasoning skills within the student. The fine arts enrich literature and history courses, while government and economics are taught by master teachers. Mathematics courses, including Precalculus and AP Calculus (Advanced Placement Calculus), and Earth Science and three lab sciences including AP Physics, comprise the Advanced Study Diploma curriculum. Drama, fine art, chorus, and orchestra are included along with an athletic program to complete the high school curriculum.

The purpose of the Noah Plan curriculum centers on first inspiring a love of learning and building up of skills by expanding the student's strong qualities, broadening and sharpening scholarship, and encouraging the student towards a fuller and more excellent expression of his value in Christ. Subject areas are taught in light of how they were used to advance the Gospel. In addition, the principles of Christian liberty, self-government, property, and union for the individual are stressed.

©2013 The Foundation for American Christian Education

Curriculum Scope and Sequence

Kindergarten	First Grade	Second Grade
Bible: Immediacy of Jesus Christ, Old Testament history, Bible literature & wisdom, New Testament history, Prayer & praise English: Sowing the seeds of the love of language through literature, composition, syntax, & language appreciation Reading: Reading readiness; Speech sound (phoneme awareness); Systematic explicit phonics—*The Writing Road to Reading*; Oral language skills—listening comprehension, expressive language; Reading fluency & comprehension; Indirect & direct vocabulary learning; Bible as a Reader Literature: Bible as literature; Poetry of Isaac Watts; Children's poets; Lullabies; *Winnie the Pooh; Aesop's Fables; Uncle Remus; Tales from Shakespeare;* d'Aulaire's *Abraham Lincoln*; Notebook Approach—*Bambi, Little House in the Big Woods*; Special Day: "Pioneer Day" History: God's Principle of Individuality; Christ, "His" Story, Timeline of Providential History: Creation Link; Pilgrims & Indians; Columbus; Patriots; Symbols of Liberty Geography: Biblical foundation; The Earth's elements; Introductory map skills; Geographic terms; Continents of history & nature; your State Arithmetic: *RightStart*™; *Activities for Learning*; Biblical principles; Subject principles; Thinking mathematically; Art of compu-tation; Oral, mental, visual, kinesthetic, & linguistic activities Science: The nature and character of God in all branches of science Modern Language: French The Fine & Performing Arts: Music & art appreciation; Singing & rhythm instruments; Art practice & crafts Physical Education	Bible: Immediacy of Jesus Christ, Old Testament history, Bible literature & wisdom, New Testament history, Prayer & praise English: Foundations of English, etymology, syntax, composition, elocution Reading: Systematic explicit phonics—*The Writing Road to Reading*; Oral language skills—listening comprehension, expressive lan-guage; Reading fluency & comprehension; Comprehension reinforced through composition; Indirect & direct vocabulary learning; Comprehension strategy instruction; Bible as a Reader Literature: Bible as literature; *Pinocchio*; Special Day: "Italy Day"; Children's poets; *Abigail Adams; Cinnabar;* Shakespeare's *Romeo and Juliet* History: "Conscience is the most sacred of all property."; The Chain of Christianity®: Columbus Link Geography: The Map Standard; Geographic terms; Physical Geography of the seven continents Arithmetic: *RightStart*™; *Activities for Learning*; Biblical principles; Subject principles; Thinking mathematically; Art of compu-tation; Oral, mental, visual, kinesthetic, & linguistic activities Science: The nature and character of God and His principles in Chemistry, Physics, Meteorology, and Oceanography; Experiments & observations Modern Language: French The Fine & Performing Arts: Music & art appreciation; Singing & rhythm instruments; Art practice & crafts Physical Education	Bible: Immediacy of Jesus Christ, Old Testament history, Bible literature & wisdom, New Testament history, Prayer & praise English: Foundations of English, etymology, syntax, composition, elocution Reading: Systematic phonics instruction; Oral language skills—listening comprehension, expressive language; Reading fluency & comprehension; Comprehension reinforced through composition; Indirect & direct vocabulary learning; Comprehension strategy instruction; Bible as a Reader Literature: Bible as literature; Children's poets; *Benjamin West; Heidi*; Special Day: "Heidi Day"; *Pocahontas;* Shakespeare's *Comedy of Errors; Benjamin Franklin* History: The Principle of Christian Self-Government; The Chain of Christianity®: Bible in English Link Geography: The Map Standard; Geographic terms; Land masses; Physical & political study of North America; Virginia Arithmetic: *RightStart*™; *Activities for Learning*; Biblical principles; Subject principles; Thinking mathematically; Art of computation; Oral, mental, visual, kinesthetic, & linguistic activities Science: The nature and character of God and His principles in Geology, Botany, Astronomy; Experiments & observations Modern Language: French The Fine & Performing Arts: Music & art appreciation; Singing & rhythm instruments; Art practice & crafts Physical Education

©2013 The Foundation for American Christian Education

Curriculum Scope and Sequence

THIRD GRADE	FOURTH GRADE	FIFTH GRADE
BIBLE: Immediacy of Jesus Christ, Old Testament history, Bible literature & wisdom, New Testament history, Prayer & praise ENGLISH: Foundations of English, etymology, syntax, composition, elocution READING: Systematic phonics instruction; Reading fluency & comprehension; Comprehension reinforced through composition; Indirect & direct vocabulary learning; Comprehension strategy instruction; Bible as a Reader LITERATURE: Bible as literature; Children's poets; *Hans Brinker*; Special Days: "Hans Brinker Day" & "Bach Tea"; *Johann Sebastian Bach; The Lion, the Witch, & the Wardrobe;* Shakespeare's *Merchant of Venice* HISTORY: The Principle of Christian Character; The Chain of Christianity®: American Founding Link GEOGRAPHY: The Map Standard; Geographic terms; Physical & political study of Europe, England, The Netherlands, & Germany ARITHMETIC: *RightStart™*; *Activities for Learning*; Biblical principles; Subject principles; Thinking mathematically; Art of computation; Oral, mental, visual, kinesthetic, and linguistic activities SCIENCE: The nature and character of God and His principles in Zoology, Anatomy & Physiology; Experiments & observations MODERN LANGUAGE: French FINE & PERFORMING ARTS: Music & art appreciation; Singing & rhythm instruments; Art practice & crafts; Drama PHYSICAL EDUCATION	BIBLE: Immediacy of Jesus Christ, Old Testament history, Bible literature & wisdom, New Testament history, Prayer & praise ENGLISH: Foundations of English, etymology, syntax, composition, elocution; colonial essay READING: Reading to learn—refinement & improvement; Latin-roots & multiple meanings of vocabulary; Strategic reading process; Reasoning & reading; Timed readings; Comprehension reinforced through composition; Bible as a Reader LITERATURE: Bible as literature; Children's poets; *Carry On, Mr. Bowditch; The Secret Garden; Treasure Island*; Special Day: "Treasure Island Day"; Shakespeare's *Julius Caesar* HISTORY: The Principle of the Christian Form of Our Government; The Chain of Christianity®: The American Christian Republic Link GEOGRAPHY: The Map Standard; Geographic terms; Physical & political study of Asia, Africa, South & Central America ARITHMETIC: *RightStart™*; *Activities for Learning*; Biblical principles; Subject principles; Thinking mathematically; Art of computation; Oral, mental, visual, kinesthetic, & linguistic activities SCIENCE: The nature and character of God and His principles in Chemistry, Physics, Meteorology, Oceanography; Experiments & observations MODERN LANGUAGE: French CLASSICAL LANGUAGE: Latin Primer FINE & PERFORMING ARTS: Music & art appreciation; Singing; Recorder; Art practice & crafts; Drama PHYSICAL EDUCATION	BIBLE: Old Testament survey ENGLISH: Foundations of English, etymology, syntax, composition, drama; research paper; Oral presentation READING: Reading to learn—refinement & improvement; Vocabulary analysis; Reading in content areas & literature; Strategic reading process; Reasoning & reading; Comprehension reinforced through composition; Bible as a Reader LITERATURE: Bible as literature; Children's poets; *Little Women*; Special Day: "Etiquette Luncheon"; *Trailblazer of the Seas; The Wind in the Willows;* Shakespeare's *Macbeth* HISTORY: The Chain of Christianity®: Expansion & Erosion Link; The Constitution; Field study tour GEOGRAPHY: The Map Standard; Geographic terms; Physical & political study of the United States & your State MATHEMATICS: *Ray's™ New Practical Arithmetic*; Biblical principles; Subject principles; Mastery & application of arithmetic skills; The science of numbers; Logical thinking SCIENCE: The nature and character of God and His principles in Geology, Botany, Astronomy; Experiments & observations MODERN LANGUAGE: French FINE & PERFORMING ARTS: Music & art appreciation; Singing; Recorder; Art practice & crafts; Drama COMPUTER SCIENCE PHYSICAL EDUCATION

©2013 The Foundation for American Christian Education

Curriculum Scope and Sequence

Sixth Grade	Seventh Grade	Eighth Grade
Bible: New Testament Survey	Bible: Christian youth leadership	Bible: Christian doctrines & creeds
English: Foundations of English, etymology, syntax, composition, drama; historical production; Oral presentation	English: Foundations of English, etymology, syntax, composition; Speech; Shakespeare drama production	English: Foundations of English, etymology, syntax, composition, drama; melodrama production; 8th grade graduation speech
Reading: Reading to learn—refinement & improvement; Vocabulary analysis; Reading in content areas & literature; Strategic reading process; Reasoning & reading; Comprehension reinforced through composition; Bible as a Reader	Reading: Analysis & enrichment in vocabulary; Reading in content areas & literature; Reasoning & writing; Bible as a Reader	Reading: Analysis & enrichment in vocabulary; Reading in content areas & literature; Reasoning & writing; Bible as a Reader
Literature: Bible as Literature; Children's poets; *Wizard of the North; Ivanhoe;* Special Day: "Ivanhoe Day"; *A Christmas Carol;* Shakespeare's *Twelfth Night*	Literature: Bible as literature; Poetry; Types of literature; *David Copperfield; Abe Lincoln Grows Up; The Farmer's Letters;* Shakespeare's *Hamlet*	Literature: Christian & pagan literature; *Cicero; Seneca; The Odyssey; The Walls of Windy Troy; Ben Hur; King Arthur* & *His Knights; Idylls of the King; Courtship of Miles Standish;* Shakespeare's *Comedy of Errors*
History: A survey of ancient, middle, & medieval history; Field study tour	History: A survey of modern history	History and Geography: Rudiments of America's Christian History & Government
Geography: The study of Geography in ancient, middle, & medieval history	Geography: A study of the geography of modern history	
Mathematics: *Ray's™ New Higher Arithmetic*; Biblical principles; Subject principles; Mastery and application of arithmetic skills; The science of numbers; Logical thinking	Mathematics: *Ray's™ New Higher Arithmetic*; Biblical principles; Subject principles; Mastery & application of arithmetic skills; The science of numbers; Logical thinking	Mathematics: Algebra I Biblical Principles; Subject Principles; Applied mathematics; Connecting abstract to concrete reality; Mastery & application of arithmetic skills; The science of numbers; Logical thinking
Science: The nature and character of God and His principles in Zoology, Anatomy & Physiology; Science project	Science: The nature and character of God and His principles in Chemistry, Physics, Meteorology, Oceanography; Science project	Science: The nature and character of God and His principles in Geology, Botany, Astronomy, Oceanography; Science project
Modern Language: French	Classical Language: Latin I	Classical Language: Latin II
Fine & Performing Arts: Music appreciation & Chorus; Art appreciation, practice, & crafts; Drama; Musical performance	Fine & Performing Arts: Music appreciation & Chorus; Art appreciation, practice, & crafts; Drama; Musical performance	Fine & Performing Arts: Music appreciation & Chorus; Art appreciation & practice; Drama
Computer Science	Computer Science	Computer Science
Physical Education	Physical Education	Physical Education

©2013 The Foundation for American Christian Education

Curriculum Scope and Sequence

NINTH GRADE	TENTH GRADE	ELEVENTH GRADE	TWELFTH GRADE
BIBLE: Introduction to the Bible; Hermeneutics and principles of sound interpretation	BIBLE: Exegetical methodology; the Old Testament Canon	BIBLE: Intertestamental background, New Testament language, Analysis of the New Testament	BIBLE: Inductive study of the Bible, Developing a Biblical perspective of identity, significance, and security
ENGLISH: English Literature 450–1660; Reading with Reason; etymology, composition, syntax	ENGLISH: English Literature 1600–present; Reading with Reason; etymology, composition, syntax	ENGLISH: American Literature 1607–1840; Reading with Reason; etymology, composition	ENGLISH: American Literature 1840–present; Reading with Reason; etymology, composition; Senior thesis
UNIVERSAL HISTORY: Pre-Christian West, Christian West & World, Creation to 1860	MODERN HISTORY: Ideas & worldviews in Western civilization, 1600 to present; Portfolio Project	UNITED STATES HISTORY: A.D. 1000 to present; Oration	HISTORY: American Government & Economics or AP Government and Economics; Senior thesis and defense
MATHEMATICS: ALGEBRA II	MATHEMATICS: GEOMETRY	MATHEMATICS: PRE-CALCULUS	MATHEMATICS: CALCULUS or AP CALCULUS
SCIENCE: Elementary Physics; Science project	SCIENCE: Chemistry; Science project	SCIENCE: Botany, Zoology; Science project	SCIENCE: AP Physics or Human Anatomy & Physiology
CLASSICAL OR MODERN LANGUAGE: French, Spanish, Greek, or Latin	CLASSICAL OR MODERN LANGUAGE: French, Spanish, Greek, or Latin	CLASSICAL OR MODERN LANGUAGE: French, Spanish, or Greek	CLASSICAL OR MODERN LANGUAGE: French, Spanish, or Greek
FINE & PERFORMING ARTS: Drama, Orchestra, Chorus, Art (elective)	FINE & PERFORMING ARTS: Drama, Orchestra, Chorus, Art (elective)	FINE & PERFORMING ARTS: Drama, Orchestra, Chorus, Art (elective)	FINE & PERFORMING ARTS: Drama, Orchestra, Chorus, Art (elective)
PHYSICAL EDUCATION	PHYSICAL EDUCATION	COMPETITIVE SPORTS	COMPETITIVE SPORTS
			CULMINATION: Senior ministry trip and Reformation tour of Europe

©2013 The Foundation for American Christian Education

—Sample Christian History Study—

Noah Webster, a Man Used of God in America's Providential History

I. Inheritance:
A. Webster's Family Heritage:

1. Father—Noah, Sr.—descended from Puritan named John Webster (came to America in 1630s and followed Thomas Hooker to CT) who became governor of CT; he was rugged, Yankee farmer, served in French & Indian War, as a deacon in a Congregational Church, and as Justice of the Peace in West Hartford; intelligent & wise; his counsel was often sought in the community.
2. Mother—Mercy Steele—great granddaughter of Gov. William Bradford of Plymouth Plantation; she was of great intelligence, gentle & loving in all her ways.
3. Noah was fourth of five children who all lived long, productive lives.
   Born: October 16, 1758 on an 80-acre farm in West Hartford, CT.
4. Married *Rebecca Greenleaf*: witty, sensible, gay, & social woman at age of 30.
5. Had seven living children (6 daughters and 1 son) whom he educated and continued a correspondence with all through life.
6. He had many grandchildren, whom he loved.

B. Providentially in Philadelphia during Constitutional Convention:
his wisdom was sought often by the delegates.

C. Converted at age of 49
and made a public confession in church in 1808 just prior to beginning his work on the *Dictionary*.

II. Character Formation:
A. Home, Family & Farm Life in Connecticut:

Lonely for children and provided long hours of work, Noah expected to perform many tasks on the farm for his father who early trained him to severe and unremitting industry: early rising, strict temperance, vigorous exercise which all prolonged Noah's life.

Connecticut enjoyed more self-government than any other colony and its Constitution was a model for the U.S. Constitution.

West Hartford—thrifty, industrious farming town

Three influences in Connecticut that shaped thinking:

a. Yankee philosophy of hard work
b. Town Meeting form of civil government
c. Congregational Church (State church)—Calvinism

Blessing from his parents upon leaving for Yale:

"We wish to have you serve your generation and do good in the world and be useful and may you so behave as to gain the esteem of all virtuous people that are acquainted with you; and gain a comfortable subsistence, but especially that you may so live as to obtain the favor of Almighty God and His grace in this world and a saving interest in the merits of Jesus Christ, without which no man can be happy."

B. Church:
His family attended the Congregational Church; active in music; father—deacon; as an adult he served in the church.

C. Education and Schooling:

Connecticut had state law requiring elementary education 11 mo./yr.

Noah attended when he wasn't needed on the farm.

Books: Psalter, KJV Bible, N. E. Primer; Christian Catechism.

Tutored for college entrance by Rev. Nathan Perkins for 2 years.

Entered Yale College at age of 15. Met G. Washington on campus.

1778—Graduated with B.A.

Read Law with Olliver Ellsworth.

1781—Admitted to the Bar.

1781—received his M.A. Degree from Yale for his dissertation.

1822—received LL.D. from Yale.

D Friends and Associates

Were all men of powerful intellect:

Noah's Yale Graduating Class—Most distinguished class until the Civil War: Joel Barlow—Poet; Alexander Wolcott & Abraham Bishop—Jefferson Compatriots; Zephaniah Swift—CT's greatest jurist; John Trumbull; Oliver Wolcott—Secretary of the Treasury; Uriah Tracy—U.S. Senator; Josiah Meigs—President of U. of Georgia

Other Friends: George Washington; John Adams; John Jay; Timothy Puckering; Benjamin Franklin; James Madison, Benjamin Rush; Alexander Hamilton

E. Noah's Hero:
"the great genius—the immortal Newton"

III. Characteristics:
A. Physical Appearance:

Tall and erect
Slender, lithe, Yankee form
Auburn hair; gray-blue eyes, square jaw
Ruddy complexion
Excellent health (but complained of ill health all his life)

B. Internal Character:

Lively disposition
Sanguine temperament (warm, ardent, and confident)
Energetic and enterprising
Lover and defender of truth
Honest
Frank in his speech
Generous with his time, counsel, & pen
Thrifty with resources
Bold, original thinker; candid mind
Witty, quick memory
Eager love for learning, loved books.
Self-confident as a leader
Polite—had a refinement of thought and feelings.
Thorough and precise
Hard-working, diligent
Self-reliant and persevering
Patriotic & passionately interested in the welfare of our country.
Had no pride of opinion—was willing to change if incorrect.
Was *The Prompter*—sat behind the scenes to correct error and assist the memory.

C. Life Time Habits:

Studied the Bible daily and prayed every morning after rising.
Maintained a daily schedule for writing, reading, and other tasks.
Set aside time each day to be with his family.

(continued, over)

– Sample Christian History Study –

Noah Webster, a Man Used of God in America's Providential History (continued)

Maintained various jobs at the same time.
Performed original investigation and research.
Arranged all his acquired knowledge in a most exact order.
Kept a daily journal.
Preserved documents carefully, filed articles he read and wrote.
Marked all new words, corrected errors in margins of his books, kept references to corresponding passages in other works.
His method was his presiding principle of life.
His son-in-law, Chauncey Goodrich, said these qualities sustained Noah through difficulties that would have crushed other men's spirits.

D. Quotes:

"Education is useless without the Bible."
"An immense effect may be produced by small powers wisely and steadily directed."
"The basis of all excellence in writing and conversation is truth—truth is intellectual gold, which is as durable as it is splendid and valuable."
"In my view, the Christian religion is the most important and one of the first things in which all children ought to be instructed."
"All government originates in families, and if neglected there, it will hardly exist in society . . . the foundation of all free government and social order must be laid in families and in the discipline of youth."

IV. Contributions:

A. Educator—America's Greatest Schoolmaster:

Educated his own children.
Taught school while he studied law.
First teacher to develop a civics course
Head, Episcopal School in Philadelphia
Simplified spelling providing principles and pronunciation.
Taught millions of Americans to read.
Taught music.

B. Founder & President, Amherst College

—Webster's Credo of Education—*Laying cornerstone at Amherst college,* 1820
"The object of this institution . . . is one of the noblest which can occupy the attention and claim the contributions of the Christian republic. It is to second the efforts of the apostles themselves, in extending and establishing the Redeemer's empire—the empire of truth. It is to aid in the important work of raising the human race from ignorance and debasement; to enlighten their minds; to exalt their character; and to teach them the way to happiness and to glory. Too long have men been engaged in the barbarous works of multiplying the miseries of human life. Too long have their exertions and resources been devoted to war and plunder; to the destruction of lives and property; to the ravage of cities; to the unnatural, the monstrous employment of enslaving and degrading their own species. Blessed be our lot! We live to see a new era in the history of man—an era when reason and religion begin to resume their sway, and to impress the heavenly truth, that the appropriate business of men, is to imitate the Savior; serve their God; and bless their fellow men."

C. Lexicographer: Recognized the American language was different than England's language and wrote first American Dictionary.

Master of over 26 languages
Made a profound study of philology and etymology of words.
Included over 70,000 words.
Took him nearly 20 years to complete (70 years old).
Wrote Biblical definitions & exhortations.
Contained scientific terms—was more like an encyclopedia.
Changed and unified spelling.
Included 20,000 new words.
Reflected America's Christian philosophy of life & government.

D. Lawyer & Judge:

Fought for and secured copyright laws in America.
Fought for uniform patent laws.
Active in anti-slavery movement.
Served as Judge in state court system.
Boston General Court member
Representative from New Haven in State legislature

E. Defender of the U.S. Constitution:

Wrote "Sketches of American Policy."
Proposed & fought for a U.S. Constitution.
Traveled around the new nation to promote the ratification.

F. Author, Editor & Publisher:

Wrote on a greater variety of topics than any other U.S. author.

Text books:

"Blue-Backed Speller"—backbone of American Education (revealed the spirit of liberty and independence for it used a self-taught method); over 100 million published by 1910—more than any other book in America.
Readers—one contained geography & history of the United States
Grammar Book
Histories
Catechism for U.S. Constitution
Introduced Biology to Children
Began a literary magazine (*American Magazine*) and *The Prompter*
He translated the Bible.

G. Natural Scientist

He compiled and wrote a *History of Epidemic Disease* which Johns Hopkins still uses today.

V. Bibliography

American Dictionary of the English Language (1828) by Noah Webster—added biography, "Noah Webster: Founding Father of American Education" by Rosalie J. Slater, F.A.C.E., 1967.

The Life and Testimony of Noah Webster, by Chauncey A. Goodrich, quoted in *Teaching and Learning America's Christian History,* Appendix, pp. 280–301.

Noah Webster: Schoolmaster to America, by Harry R. Warfel, Macmillan Co., NY, 1936.

Lesson 8

The Principle Approach®
Education for the
Twenty-First Century

The Noah Plan®
Biblical · Classical · American Education

What's Wrong?	Let's Solve It
The culture is on a crash course propelled by secular, humanistic agendas driven by modern education.	Reformation comes one soul, one heart, one mind at a time. Join the reformation of the nation!

Lesson 8 — Assignments

Readings

1. Lesson 8
2. "The PEERS Test" Trend Chart, p. 97

Reflections

1. Study the graph of "Principle Approach®" education on p. 86 and consider and ponder.
2. Carefully evaluate the Distinctives of Principle Approach Education, p. 85.

Writing

1. Compete Word Studies on "consecrated mind" and "intellectual virtue."
2. Apply definitions, principles, and distinctives gleaned from this lesson to your "Educational Philosophy Chart"; layout for photocopying found on pages 98–101.

©2013 The Foundation for American Christian Education

THE PRINCIPLE APPROACH®: EDUCATION FOR THE TWENTY-FIRST CENTURY

Let divines and philosophers, statesmen and patriots, unite their endeavors to renovate the age, by impressing the minds of men with the importance of educating their little boys and girls, of inculcating in the minds of youth the fear and love of the Deity and universal philanthropy, and, in subordination to these great principles, the love of their country; of instructing them in the art of self-government, without which they never can act a wise part in the government of societies, great or small; in short, of leading them in the study and practice of the exalted virtues of the Christian system and the art of self-government.

— Samuel Adams, Boston, October 4, 1790, *Christian History,* Vol. I, p. XIV

Principle Approach Education Distinctives:

1. Is characterized by the *supremacy of the Bible* and its teaching methodology in all instruction.
2. Applies *Biblical principles* in scholarship, reasoning, character formation, and developing Christian self-government.
3. Acknowledges *America's Christian history and Biblical form of government,* teaching them in every subject.
4. Uses Webster's 1828 *Dictionary* to provide the *vocabulary of liberty* in learning that is consistent with Biblical truth.
5. *Acknowledges parents* as those mandated by God for the education of their children and helps form homes and schools into communities of learning.
6. *Values the worth and dignity* of each student and nurtures each one to achieve his fullest potential in Christ.
7. Cultivates the *teacher to be the "living textbook."*
8. Employs a *classical, Biblical* curriculum.
9. Acknowledges *individual learning styles* and aptitude.
10. Produces a *Biblical Christian worldview.*
11. Holds the *student accountable for his learning.*
12. Places the responsibility for the character and preservation of our Christian constitutional republic upon the parent and educator by demonstrating the consistent classroom government and self-government that respond to the admo-nition of America's founding father, Sam Adams, "to teach our little boys and girls the exalted virtues of the Christian system and *the art of self-government,*" (*as quoted above; emphasis added*).

©2013 The Foundation for American Christian Education

The Principle Approach®

The Word of God at the Heart of Education

for every subject

God's Principles —The Truth
Combine spiritual thoughts with spiritual words.
—I Corinthians 2:13

Structure —The Way
I am the way, and the truth, and the life.
—John 14:6

Life
Thy word hath quickened me.
—Psalm 119:50
The word of God is living.
—Hebrews 4:12

Gospel Purpose
Lord . . . thou hast the words of eternal life.
—John 6:68

for every student

Inspiration
There is a spirit in man: and the inspiration of the Almighty gives understanding. —Job 32:8

Consecrated Mind
Be ye transformed by the renewing of your mind.
—Romans 12:2

Intellectual Virtue
Take every thought captive to the obedience of Christ.
—II Corinthians 10:5

Biblical World & Life View
Do good, be rich in good works, ready to distribute, willing to communicate, laying a good foundation . . . [for] eternal life.
—I Tim. 6:18–19

The Holy Bible
The Logos

Biblical Reasoning from God's Word

Discerning and applying
Biblical Principles in:

Art
Math
History
Science
Geography
Logic
Literature
Music
Drama
Grammar
Reading
Composition
Rhetoric
Language

Christian Character — Biblical World & Life View

The Church
Family Life
Social Life & Relationships
Invention & Technology
Communication & The Media
Public Policy
Foreign Relations
Economics
Business & Industry
Civil Government

Glorifies God

©2013 The Foundation for American Christian Education

What is the Product of American Christian Education?

American Christian Education lifts every student to the standard of Christ through the ideals of the Principle Approach®, calling forth the fullest expression of his value in Christ. As each student is instructed, mentored, and challenged with an enriched and diverse program of study, he is able to grow spiritually, academically, aesthetically, and socially. Educated to enter a world of diverse challenges with Biblical solutions, each graduate is equipped with the necessary tools to articulate and defend his worldview as an ambassador of Christ through his Christian scholarship, character, and ability to govern himself. Include the following qualities in your educational vision:

High School Graduate Ideals

Internal Qualities:

1. "To know God and Jesus Christ, which is eternal life, Joh. 17.3. and therefore, to lay Christ at the bottome as the only foundation of sound knowledge and Learning." (*New Englands First Fruits,* Harvard College, 1648)
2. To bring into captivity every thought to the obedience of Christ (II Corinthians 10:5), therefore building the foundation of Christian liberty (John 8:32).
3. To honor parents and to be prepared to build a Christian family where government and education are taught and practiced.
4. To be made complete and adequate, able to fulfill the calling and purposes of God in his life (Hebrews 13:21).
5. "To develop a wise and virtuous man, fit to be trusted with the liberty of his country" (Sam Adams, Colonial Patriot).
6. To be found capable of being an independent scholar, able to articulate a defense of the faith, and to apply Biblically-based and governmental principles, thus prepared to take dominion of domestic and civil responsibilities.

External Qualities and Skills:

Stewardship:

"Moreover, it is required of stewards that one be found trustworthy." —I Corinthians 4:2

1. To wisely govern one's personal God-given internal and external property in a manner reflecting the character of Christ.
2. To have an understanding of Christian economics and its effect on society.
3. To be properly equipped and apprenticed in a tent-making occupation, having learned the principles of an entrepreneur.
4. To embrace the Biblical work ethic as a way of life.

Scholarship:

"Study to shew thyself approved, a workman that needeth not to be ashamed, rightly dividing the word of truth." —II Timothy 2:15

1. To embrace the Word of God as the only rule for faith and practice.
2. To be able to reason Biblically and logically.
3. To demonstrate the basic skills and technology of research.
4. To have full knowledge and understanding of:
   - American's Christian history and government
   - Universal history and literature
   - The Providential Hand of God and the history of liberty in Western civilization
   - Great classical literature and languages

©2013 The Foundation for American Christian Education

- Mathematics and the sciences
- The fine and performing arts and the aesthetic components of life

5. To have mastery and an appreciation of a foreign language beginning in primary school, with an emphasis on Latin in the middle school experience, and choices of the Romantic and classical languages in high school.

Servanthood:

"Whosoever will be chief among you, let him be your servant." —Matthew 20:27

1. To demonstrate a love for God through service to others.
2. To be able to demonstrate civic concern and voluntaryism.

Statesmanship:

"We are ambassadors for Christ."
—II Corinthians 5:20

1. To honorably represent Christ, family, school, and nation.
2. To be trained in leadership skills.
3. To be able to give a defense for the hope that lies within.
4. To demonstrate vision for local and national effectiveness in witness and mission.

©2013 The Foundation for American Christian Education

Lesson 9

Your Vision

The Noah Plan®

Biblical · Classical · American Education

Your Vision

Where there is no vision, the people perish.

—Proverbs 29:18a

Write the vision and make it plain on tablets, that he may run that reads it.

—Habakkuk 2:2

❖

1. Based upon your educational philosophy, write the educational vision that God has given you in your specific calling as a pastor, a parent, a school or home educator.

2. Write the vision God has given you for your students. Develop your vision into the school brochure that reflects the components of your philosophy.

3. Write a plan with specific goals and objectives for each component.

4. Develop your ideas into a five-year plan.

©2013 The Foundation for American Christian Education

GLOSSARY

That the God of our Lord Jesus Christ, the Father of glory, may give unto you the spirit of wisdom and revelation in the knowledge of Him: the eyes of your understanding being enlightened; . . .
—Ephesians 1:17–18

Ideas are inspired by the meanings of words. Following are some definitions of the vocabulary of liberty in learning from the *American Dictionary of the English Language* by Noah Webster, 1828:

1. **believe**, v.t. [Saxon, geleaf leave.]
   To credit upon the authority or testimony of another; to be persuaded of the truth of something upon the declaration of another or upon evidence furnished by reasons, arguments, and deductions of the mind, or by other circumstances than personal knowledge. When we believe upon the authority of another, we always put confidence in his veracity. When we believe upon the authority of reasoning, arguments, or a concurrence of facts and circumstances, we rest our conclusions upon their strength of probability, their agreement with our own experience.

2. **critical**, adj. Capable of judging with accuracy.

3. **govern**, v.t.
   a. To direct and control, as the actions or conduct of men, either by established laws or by arbitrary will; to regulate by authority; to keep within the limits prescribed by law or sovereign will. Thus in free states, men are governed by the constitution and laws; in despotic states, men are governed by the edicts or commands of a monarch. Every man should govern well his own family.
   b. To regulate; to influence; to direct.
   c. To control; to restrain.

4. **idea**, n. [L. idea, from Gk. meaning to see.]
   a. Literally, that which is seen; hence, form, image, model of any thing in the mind; that which is held or comprehended by the understanding or intellec-tual faculties. The attention of the understanding to the objects acting on it, by which it becomes sensible of the impressions they make, is called by logicians, perception; and the notices themselves as they exist in the mind, as the materials of thinking and knowledge, are distinguished by the name, ideas. (Ency. art. Logic)
   b. Image in the mind.

5. **illuminate**, v.t. [Fr. illuminer; L. in and lumino light; to enlighten.]
   a. To enlighten; to throw light on; to supply with light.
   b. To enlighten intellectually with knowledge or grace. (Heb. 10:13)
   c. To illustrate; to throw light on, as on obscure subjects. Watts.

6. **imagination**, n. The power or faculty of the mind by which it conceives and forms ideas of things communicated to it by the senses. We would define imagination to be the will working on the materials of memory; not satisfied with following the order prescribed by nature, or suggested by accident.

7. **imagine**, v.i. [L. imaginor, from imago, image.]
   a. To form a notion or idea in the mind; to fancy.
   b. To form ideas or representations in the mind, by modifying and combining our conceptions.
   c. To contrive in purpose; to scheme, to devise.

8. **inspire**, v.t. [L. inspiro; in and spiro to breathe.]
   a. To breathe into.
   b. To infuse by breathing.

©2013 The Foundation for American Christian Education

c. To infuse into the mind; as, to inspire with new life.
d. To infuse or suggest ideas or monitions supernaturally; to communicate divine instructions to the mind. In this manner, we suppose the prophets to have been inspired, and the Scriptures to have been composed under divine influence or direction.

9. **intellect**, n. [L. intelligo to understand.] That faculty of the human soul or mind, which receives or comprehends the ideas communicated to it by the senses or by perception, or by other means; the faculty of thinking; otherwise called the understanding. A dear intellect receives and entertains the same ideas which another communicates with perspicuity.

10. **judge**, v.i. [Fr. jugement.]
   a. The act of judging; the act or process of the mind in comparing its ideas, to find their agreement or disagreement, and to ascertain truth; or the process of examining facts and arguments, to ascertain propriety and justice; or the process of examining the relations between one proposition and another.
   b. The faculty of the mind by which man is enabled to compare ideas and ascertain the relations of terms and propositions as a man of dear judgment or sound judgment. The judgment may be biased by prejudice. Judgment supplies the want of certain knowledge.
   c. The determination of the mind, formed from comparing the relations of ideas, or the comparison of facts and arguments. In the formation of our judgments, we should be careful to weigh and compare all the facts connected with the subject.

11. **just**, adj. [Fr. juste; L. justus. The primary sense is probably straight or close, from the sense of setting, erecting, or extending.]
   a. Regular; orderly; due; suitable.
   b. Exactly proportioned; proper.
   c. In a moral sense, upright; honest; having principles of rectitude; or conforming exactly to the laws, and to principles of rectitude in social conduct; equitable in the distribution of justice; as a just judge.
   d. In an evangelical sense, righteous; religious; influenced by a regard to the laws of God; or living in exact conformity to the divine will. There is not a just man on earth, that doeth good and sinneth not (Ec. 7).
   e. Conformed to rules of justice. Just balances, just weights, a just ephah and a just hin shall ye have (Lev. 19).
   f. True; founded in truth and fact.
   g. Innocent; blameless; without guilt. How could man be just with God? (Job 9).
   h. Equitable; due; merited; as a just recompense or reward. Whose damnation is just? (Ro. 3).
   i. Exactly; nicely; accurately.

12. **learn**, v.t. [Sax. leornian and laeran, to teach, the same word having both significations, to teach and to learn.]
   a. To gain knowledge of; to acquire knowledge or ideas of something before unknown. We learn the use of letters, the meaning of words and the principles of science. We learn things by instruction, by study, and by experience and observation. It is much easier to learn what is right, than to unlearn what is wrong. Now learn the parable of the fig tree (Matt. 24).
   b. To acquire skill in any thing; to gain by practice a faculty of performing; as, to learn to play on a flute or an organ. The chief art of learning is to attempt but little at a time. Locke.
   c. To teach; to communicate the knowledge of something before unknown.

13. **meditate**, v.i.
   To dwell on anything in thought; to contemplate; to study; to turn or revolve any subject in the mind; appropriately but not exclusively used of pious contemplation, or a consideration of the great truths of religion. His delight is in the law of the Lord and in his law doth he meditate day and night (Ps. 1).

14. **memory**, n. [L. memoria, from the Gk. root for mind.] The faculty of the mind by which it retains the knowledge of past events, or ideas which are past.

15. **mind**, n. [Saxon gemind L. reminisor; L. mens; Gk. mind ardor of mind; Sans. mans, mana; mind, heart, thought. Mind signifies properly intention, a reaching or inclining forward to an object.]
   a. Intention; purpose; design (Prov 21).

©2013 The Foundation for American Christian Education

b. Inclination; will; desire.
c. Opinion.
d. Memory; remembrance.
e. The intellectual or intelligent power in man; the understanding; the power that conceives, judges or reasons. So we speak of a sound mind, a disordered mind, a weak mind, a strong mind, with reference to the active powers of the understanding; and in a passive sense, it denotes capacity, as when we say, the mind cannot comprehend a subject.
f. The heart or seat of affection. Which were a grief of mind to Isaac and Rebekah (Gen. 26).
g. The will and affection; as readiness of mind (Acts 22).
h. The implanted principle of grace (Ro. 7).

16. **muse**, v.i. [Fr. muser, to loiter or trifle.]
a. To ponder; to think closely; to study in silence. I muse on the works of thy hands (Ps. 148).
b. To wonder.

17. **perspicuity**, n. [L. per and speculum, a glass.] Clearness to mental vision; easiness to be understood; freedom from obscurity or ambiguity; that quality of writing or language which readily presents to the mind of another the precise ideas of the author. Perspicuity is the first excellence of writing or speaking.

18. **philosophy**, n. [Gk. to love and wisdom; L. philosophia.]
a. Literally, the love of wisdom. But in modern acceptation, philosophy is a general term denoting an explanation of the reason of things; or an investigation of the causes of all phenomena both of mind and of matter.
b. Reasoning; argumentation.

19. **ponder**, v.t. [L. pondero, from pondo, a pound, to weigh; Persian banazidan, to think, to consider.]
a. To weigh in the mind; to consider and compare the circumstances or consequences of an event, or the importance of the reasons for or against a decision. Mary kept all these things, and pondered them in her heart (Lu. 2).
b. To view with deliberation; to examine. Ponder the path of thy feet (Proverbs 9). The Lord pondereth the hearts (Prov. 21).

20. **principle**, n. [L. principium, beginning.]
a. In a general sense, the cause, source or origin of any thing; that from which a thing proceeds; as the principle motion; the principles of action.
b. Element, constituent part; primordial substance.
c. Being that produces any thing; operative cause.
d. In science, a truth admitted either without proof, or considered as having been before proved.
e. Ground; foundation; that which supports an assertion, an action, or a series of actions or reasoning.
f. A general truth.
g. A tenet; that which is believed, whether truth or not.

21. **reason**, n. [Fr. raison, L. ratio. Primarily, reason is that which is uttered.]
a. That which is thought or which is alleged in words, as the ground or cause of opinion, conclusion or determination.
b. The cause, ground, principle or motive of any thing said or done; that which supports or justifies a determination, plan or measure. "Virtue and vice are not arbitrary things; but there is a natural and eternal reason for that goodness and virtue, and against vice and wickedness." —Tillotson. (1 Pet. 3).
c. A faculty of the mind by which it distinguishes truth from falsehood, and good from evil, and which enables the possessor to deduce inferences from facts or from propositions.

22. **reason**, v.i.
a. To exercise the faculty of reason; to deduce inferences justly from premises. Brutes do not reason; children reason imperfectly.
b. To argue; to infer conclusions from premises, or to deduce new or unknown propositions from previous propositions which are known or evident.

23. **reflect**, v.i. [L. rejlecto to bend back.]
a. To throw back light; to return rays or beams.
b. To bend back.
c. To throw or turn back the thoughts upon the past operations of the mind or on past events.
d. To consider attentively; to revolve in the mind; to contemplate.

©2013 The Foundation for American Christian Education

24. **research**, v.t. [Fr. recherche.]
    a. To search or examine with continued care; to seek diligently for the truth.
    b. To search again; examine anew.

25. **teach**, v.t. [Sax. tocean, to teach, and to take]
    a. To instruct; to inform; to communicate to another the knowledge of that of which he was before ignorant. He will teach us his ways, and we will walk in his paths (Is. 2).
    b. To deliver any doctrine, art, principles or words for instruction.
    c. To tell; to give intelligence.
    d. To instruct, or to practice the business of an instructor.
    e. To suggest to the mind. For the Holy Spirit shall teach you in that same hour what ye ought to say (Luke 12).

26. **think**, v.i. [Saxon root thincan; L. duco to lead; The sense seems to be to set in the mind, or to draw out, as in meditation.]
    a. To have the mind occupied on some subject; to have ideas, or to revolve ideas in the mind.
    b. To judge; to conclude; to hold as a settled opinion (Num. 36).
    c. To intend (Num. 14).
    d. To imagine; to suppose; to fancy.
    e. To muse; to meditate. While Peter thought on the vision. . . . (Acts 10).
    f. To reflect; to recollect or call to mind. And when Peter thought thereon, he wept. (Mk. 14).
    g. To presume. Think not to say within yourselves, we have Abraham for our father (Mat. 3).
    h. To believe; to esteem; to muse on; to meditate upon. If there be any virtue, and if there be any praise, think on these things (Phil. 4).
    i. To light on by meditation.

27. **thought**, n. [Saxon, theaht, the past participle of think.]
    a. Properly, that which the mind thinks. Thought is either the act or operation of the mind, when attending to a particular subject or thing, or it is the idea consequent on that operation.
    b. Idea; conception.
    c. Fancy; conceit; something framed by the imagination.
    d. Reflection; particular consideration.
    e. Meditation; serious consideration.
    f. Design; purpose. All their thoughts are against me for evil (Ps. 56).
    g. Silent contemplation.
    h. Solicitude; care; concern.
    i. Inward reasoning; the workings of conscience. Their thoughts the meanwhile accusing or else excusing one another (Ro. 2).

28. **understanding**, n. [under and stand. The sense is to support or hold in the mind.] The faculty of the human mind by which it apprehends the real state of things presented to it, or by which it receives or comprehends the ideas which others express and intend to communicate. The understanding is called also the intellectual faculty. It is the faculty by means of which we obtain a great part of our knowledge. (Luke 24) And they said one to another, Did not our hearts burn within us, while he talked with us by the way and while he opened to us the scriptures (Luke 4:32). That the God of our Lord Jesus Christ, the Father of glory may give unto you the spirit of wisdom and revelation in the knowledge of him: the eyes of your understanding being enlightened. (Eph. 1:17 & 18b)

29. **wisdom**, n. [Saxon wise and dom.]
    a. Properly having knowledge; hence, having the power of discerning and judging correctly, or of discriminating between what is true and what is false; between what is fit and proper, and what is improper. Solomon was deemed the wisest man. But a man may be speculatively and not practically wise.
    b. Discrete and judicious in the use or application of knowledge; choosing laudable ends, and the best means to accomplish them. This is to be practically wise. (Gen. 49)
    c. Skillful; dexterous. They are wise to do evil but to do good they have no knowledge (Jer. 4).
    d. Learned; knowing; as the wise and the unwise. (Ro. 1)
    e. Godly, pious. (Prov. 13) The holy Scriptures, which are able to make thee wise to salvation (I Tim. 3).
    f. Skilled in arts, science, philosophy, or in magic and divination. (ii Sam. 14)

©2013 The Foundation for American Christian Education

HOW TO USE THE NOAH PLAN®

Noah's books were an ark *in which the American Christian spirit rode the deluge of rising anti-Christian and anti-republican waters which threatened so often to inundate the nation.*

—Rosalie J. Slater, "Noah Webster: Founding Father of American Scholarship and Education"

The joy of Principle Approach® curriculum is the liberty it affords the teacher and learner to bypass much of the "dead wood" of modern education and to go right to the heart of subjects and scholarship. Learn-ing is natural. Learning is satisfying. Real learning is spontaneous and unaffected, springing fresh from inspiration, and exercising the learner's God-designed abilities, affections, intuitions, and inclinations.

The Principle Approach is America's historic method of education that makes the Word of God the basis of every subject in the curriculum. Each subject begins with principles into which the facts are woven, forming through every subject a perfect tapestry of knowledge with Christ at the base.

The Noah Plan is a complete educational program designed to liberate the teacher and learner to practice Principle Approach education by the use of *guides* and *guidelines*. The important point is that *The Noah Plan* is not a set-in-stone curricular mandate that insists upon lock-step compliance to achieve the desired results. It is a *guide* that liberates both the teacher and learner to higher planes to practice education as defined by Noah Webster: "all that series of discipline and instruction that enlightens the mind, corrects the temper, forms the habits and manners of youth, and fits them for usefulness in their future stations." It is a road map to be used by both the teacher and the learner to set out on the adventure of appropriating the knowledge of God toward a sound and complete education. A *guide* is defined as a "director, a regulator, that which leads or conducts."

The teacher using *The Noah Plan* will be guided to practice the Notebook Approach for his own preparation. He will use the grade-level guidelines and the curriculum guides to acquire the best books and materials for the journey He will be a student himself, becoming for his students a lively textbook—a teacher who loves to learn and who imparts the joy and satisfaction that only a master of a subject can impart. Does this sound difficult, even intimidating? A teacher must first be a learner and a scholar, because the "pupil is not above his teacher; but everyone after he has been fully trained, will be like his teacher." (Luke 6:40)

The classroom teacher will find the subject curriculum guides and grade-level guidelines complete, and, used with the tools provided, practical and easily applied. The sample goal sheets and lesson plans give detailed models of actual use. The homeschooling parent will find the Principle Approach, as set forth in *The Noah Plan,* easily adaptable for multiple grades. For instance, a home school with second, fifth, and eighth grade students, could select topics and classics that all three levels could study in varying depths. Older students can present to younger students and vice versa. The joy of sharing an area of interest and productivity has immeasurable worth in the classroom dynamic.

Many books are required for use with *The Noah Plan* that accumulate to form a small library of the very best books ever written. The King James Bible is used for its literary quality in memorizing Scripture and in study except where other versions are specifically named for particular purposes. The Noah Webster 1828 *American Dictionary of the English Language* is used by teacher and student; however, lesser elementary dictionaries are suggested for

©2013 The Foundation for American Christian Education

the primary school beginner who is learning basic dictionary skills.

The school that implements *The Noah Plan*® can provide training for faculty by using the "Self-Directed Seminar" in the program notebook. Other valuable tools are available for use in schools—*The School Resource Guide, Christian History Study Group Packet, Beginnings in the Principle Approach*®, in addition to the study guides to the basic volumes. F.A.C.E. provides programs for schools who sponsor local seminars to introduce faculties and parents to the Principle Approach.

The homeschool parent can join a support group or association and find others in the community who are Principle Approachers. The Christian History Study Group is an excellent way to begin a new association. Training is offered by The Slater Institute. See web page at www.face.net.

We welcome you to a grand adventure in education that forever changes the spirit of teaching and learning. May you attain the mind-set of the Dutch scholar and theologian, Desiderius Erasmus, who said:

> *To be a schoolmaster is next to being a king. Do you count it a mean employment to imbue the minds of your fellow citizens in their earnest years with the best literature and with the love of Christ, and to return them to their country honest and virtuous men? In the opinion of fools, it is a humble task, but in fact it is the no lest of occupations.*

Steps for Beginning to Use *The Noah Plan*® *Lessons* Books

1. **How do I get prepared?**
   - Get a 3-ring binder to begin a teacher notebook.
   - File your notes and assignments for the *Noah Plan Self-Directed Seminar* (NPSDS) behind a divider in the teacher notebook for future reference.
   - Complete the study of the NPSDS which gives you:
     - the background necessary to practice the Principle Approach philosophy,
     - the methodology and the curriculum,
     - the familiarity with the reference volumes as you complete your lessons.
   - Allow several weeks to complete this study.
   - Make a page in the teacher notebook for recording your questions as you begin to use the *Noah Plan Lessons* books.

     (Your questions will be answered as you progress through the materials.)
2. **What do I need to collect and organize?**
   - Collect the essential materials, supplementary resources, and supplies you will need. (See "Getting Ready" chapter.)
   - Put dividers in your teacher notebook for each subject you will be teaching.
   - File your research and other collected information in your teacher notebook.
   - Organize your classroom with the tools you will need to support your curriculum: Noah Plan Wall Timeline, map, globe, etc.
   - Use the sample schedule or devise one that works well for you. The day should be orderly and comfortably paced.
3. **What will help me to visualize the program?**
   - Read the Noah Plan subject overviews to get the whole picture for the entire curriculum. (*NP Lessons* books or CDs, "Supplemental Information")
   - Select any subject and read its lessons for one quarter to get a sense of the flow of instruction and student response moving toward personal ownership.
   - Discover how all the Noah Plan books are cross-referenced.
4. **What do I do next?**
   - Follow the directions for the beginning lessons of each subject in the *Noah Plan Lessons* books

     Bible/Bible as Reader (BAR);

     Math; English; Literature; History;

     Geography; Science
   - Later you might see the need to set up separate notebooks for each subject.

©2013 The Foundation for American Christian Education

PEERS Trend Chart

(Based on worldview testing of approximately 90,000 students in 1,000 schools)

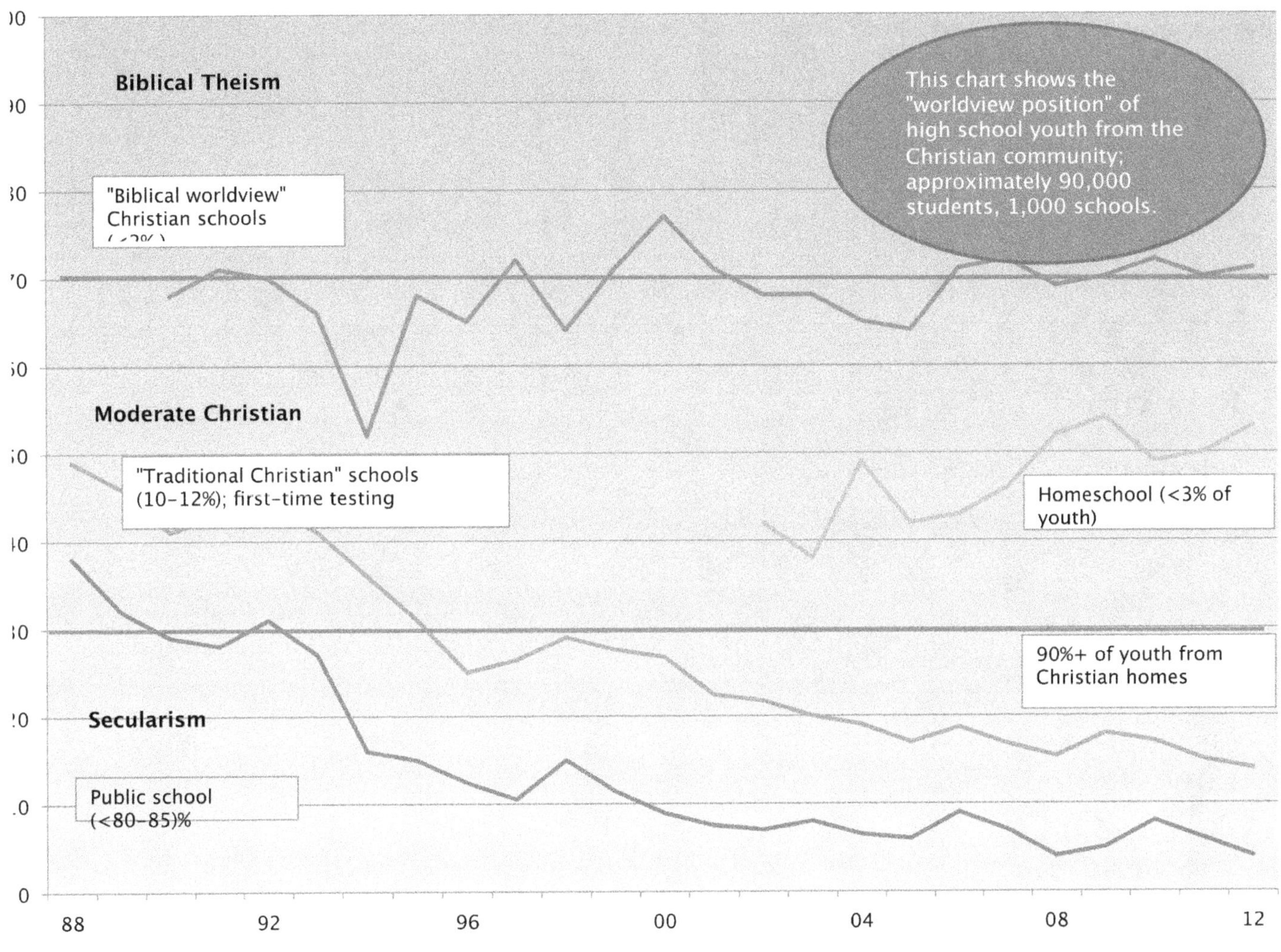

The research was conducted by Nehemiah Institute between 1988 and 2012. The results indicate that the ability to reason from a Biblical worldview increases annually among Principle Approach students, while it declines among Christian students in traditional Christian schools and in public schools, as well as homeschool students. This "trend" chart has alarming implications for the next generation.

©2013 The Foundation for American Christian Education

LEADING IDEA	DEFINITIONS
1. PURPOSES OF EDUCATION a. To know God fully b. To be filled with the knowledge of His will c. To be equipped for every good work d. To make disciples for Christ	
2. NATURE OF EDUCATION a. Instruction b. Discipline	
3. OBJECTIVES OF EDUCATION a. Enlighten the understanding b. Correct the temper c. Form the manners and habits of youth d. Fit him for usefulness for the future	
4. THE PARENTS	PARENT: "A father or mother; he or she that produces young. The duties of *parents* to their children are to maintain, protect, and educate them." —Webster's 1828 *Dictionary* RESPONSIBILITY: "The state of being accountable for a trust." —Webster's 1828 *Dictionary*

Philosophy of Education

Biblical Principles	Applying the Leading Idea
Parents Are: 1. God's chosen teachers for their children 2. Mandated to teach their children in the admonition and love of Jesus Christ 3. To bear responsibility for building Christian character that fully represents Christ 4. To nurture and guide their children toward their full potential in Christ	1. Parents' duty to educate should not be abdicated nor usurped. 2. Education requires from parents a daily investment of time and plan for instruction in the home. 3. Parents are the "first model" of the character of Christ—the "living" curriculum. 4. When placing children in the hands of a school or tutor, parents should remain active and involved. 5. The parents' voice should be sought and honored by the school or tutor in all decisions that affect the child.

May be photocopied for use as a worksheet.

LEADING IDEA	DEFINITIONS
5. THE TEACHER	
6. THE STUDENT	
7. THE CURRICULUM	
8. THE METHODS	

 THE NOAH PLAN® © 1997, 2004, 2013, THE FOUNDATION FOR AMERICAN CHRISTIAN EDUCATION

Philosophy of Education

Biblical Principles	Applying the Leading Idea

May be photocopied for use as a worksheet.

Part II

Essential Studies in the Christian History Volumes:

Reclaiming an Abandoned Heritage

The Noah Plan®
Biblical • Classical • American Education

A Beginning Study in the Christian History Books to Obtain Four Basic Understandings

The following four Basic Understandings are brief outlines of the distinctive ideas that frame The Principle Approach® as a system of education This abbreviated presentation of the ideas is given only to suggest the distinctives and in no way to offer an exhaustive definition. Realizing the incompleteness of such a brief introduction, the reader is urged to do the further reading suggested in the primary volumes and in the Scripture. Begin with the reading and reflecting suggested here.

The Whole View of Providential History

The love of God for individuals and individual nations is made visible in the Chain of Christianity® which shows the impact of the Gospel as it moves westward through geography and history.

God's revelation of liberty with law—first personal individual Christian liberty, then civil liberty and its imprint upon nations—is seen in every subject area.

Read the *Christian History of the Constitution of the United States of America:* Volume 1, *Christian Self-Government,* "The Christian Idea of Man and Government," pp. 1–2, and the Chain of Christianity® Chart on p. 6A.

The whole view of Providential history places us as individuals on the "Chain" to identify the realities of God's purpose in our place and moment of His Story. This gives purpose, relevance, and orientation for our present lives in Christ, for the teaching of every subject, and for our relationship to the child and family.

Identify your place on the chain. What has gone before you that affects your place? What is your personal providential history—the way God has providentially prepared you for the place you now occupy?

For the teacher called to restore American Christian education, this means "do and teach," *restoring ourselves first intellectually and spiritually, then teaching the generation.*

> *For Ezra had prepared his heart to seek the law of the Lord, and to do it, and to teach in Israel statutes and judgments.* —Ezra 7:10

What does your personal restoration entail? Spiritually? Intellectually?

©2013 The Foundation for American Christian Education

REASONING FROM BIBLICAL PRINCIPLES AND LEADING IDEAS

The Principles and Leading Ideas inherent in American Christian education are Biblical, thus governmental; God is the sovereign of the universe, thus the principles of His Word are our governing principles. The chart of the principles and their expanded context in Christian history are found on pp. 112–136 in *Teaching and Learning America's Christian History: The Principle Approach®*, by Rosalie J. Slater, Foundation for American Christian Education, San Francisco, California, 1965.

Working Definitions:

A principle is the cause, source or origin of anything. It is that from which a thing proceeds, an element, a general truth.

A Leading Idea is an idea that leads the reason down a pathway of thinking.

The Biblical principles and leading ideas that relate to education and that are stated through the windows of providential history and liberty with law are:

	LEADING IDEA	ITS PRINCIPLE
FIRST:	*The Christian Idea of Man, Government, and Child*	God's Principle of Individuality
SECOND:	*The Chain of Christianity® Moves Westward*	Christian Self-Government
THIRD:	*The Principle of Representation*	"Conscience Is the Most Sacred of All Property."
FOURTH:	*The Republicanism of Christianity*	America's Heritage of Christian Character
FIFTH:	*The Bible in English*	How the Seed of Local Self-Government Is Planted
SIXTH:	*Christian Rights and English Law*	The Christian Form of Government
SEVENTH:	*Principles of Christianity & Government, "A Biblical-Political Index to John Locke"*	The Christian Principle of American Political Union

(See *Teaching & Learning*, pp. 303–366, "Christian History Study Course," for a lesson-by-lesson study program of the Leading Ideas of America's Christian History & Education)

©2013 The Foundation for American Christian Education

Applying Providential History and Biblical Principles to Curriculum and Method

Each subject must be identified by a whole view—a providential view of the subject—and must be taught by its unique principles and purposes.

Principle Approach® Curriculum:

Working Definition: Curriculum is the whole body of courses offered. It is a methodical series or order of principles in arts or sciences, for illustration or instruction.

- To identify the principles of the subject, begin by researching and defining the vocabulary of the subject in Noah Webster's 1828 *American Dictionary of the English Language* and identifying the Biblical foundations of the subject in the scripture. These definitions give insight into the structure of the subject for overviewing and lesson planning.
- Each subject has its own history and key individuals through which the subject was developed. This history of the subject shows its purpose and meaning; biographies of key individuals give the subject depth, color, and an inspiring point of contact for the student.
- Various subjects relate to each other; a whole study of the subject brings in all related fields and helps to show how the subject advanced the Gospel and liberty.
- Subjects are selected by their contribution to forming the most excellent character and abili-ties of the child—planting the seeds of all learn-ing in kindergarten; cultivating through primary school; maturing and guiding through middle school; expressing independent learning through high school.

Principle Approach Methodology:

Working Definition: Methodology is the way, manner, or order in which the curriculum is taught. Methodology is governed by the philosophy of education.

- The subjects must be researched, reasoned, related, and recorded by the student under the teacher's inspiration and governance. The student must express the subject personally.
- Every aspect of the methodology impacts the character of the student. The teacher governs the methodology which forms the character of the student.
- The method must conform to this ideal:

"educating . . . little boys and girls . . . inculcating in the minds of youth the fear and love of the Deity and universal philanthropy, and in subordination to these great principles, the love of their country; of instructing them in the art of self-government, without which they never can act a wise part in the government of societies, great or small; in short, of leading them in the study and practice of the exalted virtues of the Christian system and the art of self-government."

—Samuel Adams, Boston, October 4, 1790

©2013 The Foundation for American Christian Education

A NEW VIEW OF LEARNING: THE CHRISTIAN IDEA OF THE CHILD

Read and Reflect:

Genesis 1:27

Matthew 18:1–10

Ephesians 2:1–22

We find ourselves as parents and teachers as the products of a method of education that grew out of a secular, atheistic, evolutionary view of man and of the child. Modern Christian education, a phenomenon of this generation, attempts to "Christianize" education by coating it with Christianity, when what is needed is a whole new form.

The Principle Approach® of American Christian Education, a method that proceeds from Biblical principles as the course of its philosophy, methodology, and curriculum, is documented in *Teaching and Learning America's Christian History,* the original presentation of the Principle Approach written by Rosalie J. Slater.

Principle Approach education methods are distinctive because they proceed from the Christian idea of the child and include both content mastery and the satisfaction of the real needs of children. A visit to a Principle Approach classroom reveals a teaching and learning dynamic that presupposes the value of the individual child who bears the image of God. The classroom represents an elevation of spirit and an appreciation of learning and reasoning. The teacher is the living textbook, and the students become the producers of their own learning, as they are inspired, principled, and as they are brought nearer the fullest expression of their individual value in Christ.

Education as defined by the father of American Christian education, Noah Webster, is "all that series of instruction and discipline which is intended to enlighten the understanding, correct the temper, form the manners and habits of youth, and fit them for usefulness in their future stations." To this definition Webster adds a small sermon for our benefit: "To give children a good education in manners, arts and science, is important; to give them a religious education in indispensable; and an immense responsibility rests on parents and guardians who neglect these duties." The word *religious*, in Webster's day, meant the practice of Biblical Christianity in every area of life and character.

In education, this requires more than spreading a Christian vocabulary over the old wineskin of progressive education. It requires the restructuring of education, creating a new wineskin: the identification and application of Biblical principles in every subject and as a yardstick for choice of methods used.

> *And no one puts new wine into old wineskins; otherwise the new wine will burst the skins and it will be spilled out, and the skins will be ruined.* —Luke 5:37

("The Christian Idea of the Child," by Carole G. Adams, originally in the F.A.C.E. *Journal*, Vol. II, has been revised and republished in *Family and the Nation: Biblical Childhood*, F.A.C.E., 2002.)

©2013 The Foundation for American Christian Education

Beginning with the Christian History Books

Essential Studies for the Beginner in the Basic Volumes

How to Begin with the 1828 *American Dictionary of the English Language*

1. Define the vocabulary of your subject(s).
2. Use it consistently for word studies in your personal Bible study to develop precision of thinking and expression and to purge your vocabulary of secularism.
3. Read the Webster biography and teach it. Noah Webster is the father of American scholarship and education.
4. Define the words that challenge your life and teaching such as:

discipline	learn	create	persevere
government	teach	encourage	etc.

5. Use it in the classroom and around the dinner table as a ready reference.

How to Begin with ***The Christian History of the Constitution of the United States of America: Christian Self-Government***

This is the primary volume containing the worldview, principles, leading ideas, reasoning, and character that make the Principle Approach®. You must study and know this book.

1. Study the Preface and the Table of Contents; learn what is in the three parts:
   "The Christian Idea of Man and Government," pp. 1–36
   "American Background in England," pp. 37–146
   "Developing the Idea of Local Self-Government," pp. 147–370
2. Study the charts on pp. 6A & 270E to understand the two forms of government.
3. Study the charts on pp. 270C & 270E to understand the two forms of government.
4. Browse in the Appendices, reading this rich resource of ideas relevant to teaching and quotable for classroom or correspondence.
5. Essential studies to record for further use in the classroom:
   a. "The Christian Idea of Man and Government," pp. 1–36
   b. "History 'Of Plimoth Plantation' by William Bradford," pp. 185–240
6. Use the General Index for reference as you develop curriculum and lesson planning.

©2013 The Foundation for American Christian Education

How to Begin with *Teaching and Learning America's Christian History: The Principle Approach®*

This is our basic guide to the Christian History of the Constitution which also contains the "text" on the Principle Approach and historical resource expanding the principles. The seven principles of American Christian education and government are the basis particularly for a study of history, geography, literature, and of other subjects as they relate. Examine the "New England First Fruits," Frontispiece, p. VII. Find the mission of American Christian education stated here.

1. Study "The Christian Home" by Rev. S. Phillips, pp. 3–37. The principles here relate also to the classroom which is an extension of the home.
2. Read "The Challenge of the Christian School," pp. 56–57.
3. Thoroughly study and record for use in practice and teaching "Teacher's Guide for Christian History: The Principle Approach to American Christian Education," pp. 88–112. This is the author's original statement of Principle Approach education.
4. Use the "Principles Expanded through the Grades," pp. 113–136, as the guide to the study of *Christian History of the Constitution* for teaching the principles.

How to Begin with *The Christian History of the American Revolution: Consider and Ponder*

This lovely blue book illustrated with the masters contains the primary sources of the Revolutionary period that represent the Biblical reasoning and principles basic to the Principle Approach.

1. Study carefully the essay in the Appendix on "The Education of John Quincy Adams." This essay is a model of the method and effect of Principle Approach education.
2. Examine the five sections of the book for use as needed:

   "Think On"—a leading idea approach to the American Revolution

   "Christian Constituents of the American Revolution"—home, church, education

   "Christian Liberty Ready to Pass to the American Strand"

   "God Prepares a People"—the accounts of the war by Warren and Ramsay

   "Arm of the Flesh or Arm of the Lord"
3. Learn to use the "Index of Leading Ideas" in the Appendix—an extraordinary tool, more than an index, for teaching in any subject. For instance, in math you might look up the word *dollar* and find its history.

©2013 The Foundation for American Christian Education

Designing Curriculum Using the Four R's

Your personal research and written record should be organized in such a way that it will enable you to teach any age group of learners. Compile your research in a three-ring binder with dividers that reflect the whole subject. This will enable you to recover your research quickly, to add to your research, or to teach the subject at any time.

Research

Suggested Organization for Compiling Research:

- Definition (Webster's 1828 *Dictionary*)
- Vocabulary of subject
- Biblical foundation
- Christian history of the subject
- Key individuals
- Key events
- Key writings
- Leading ideas from your research
- Geographic setting
- Art, music, and drama of the subject
- Inspiration for use with students
- Student activities to enliven and enrich
- Bibliography
- Contributions to the spread of the Gospel and liberty for the individual

Biographical Research Organization:

Conscience and character (internal) are always causative.

- Providential setting
- Geographic setting
- Family history
- Education
- Childhood anecdotes
- Christian influences
- Physical description
- Personality, affections, tastes
- Character qualities
- Contributions to the Gospel and liberty
- Account of life works
- A personal timeline

Additional Resources:

- *The Book of Life* (eight volumes, arranged and edited by Hall and Wood, John Rudin & Co, Inc., Chicago, preferably 1923–1952 editions)
- Primary sources and documentation
- Autobiographical materials
- Nineteenth and early twentieth century books
- Contemporary Christian authors
- *World Book Encyclopedia* (for basic information; a timeline is often available for many subjects)

Reason

Leading Ideas:

- The Biblical principles of the subject and God's purpose for it must always be deduced from God's Word using the 1828 vocabulary of the subject.
- Contributions the subject has made to the spread of the Gospel and liberty for the individual should always be identified.
- Many others present themselves as the subject is researched.

Relate

Ideas for Designing Curriculum for Your Grade Level:

Lesson Plans, Homework, Tests, Projects, Dramas

Record

Your Written Work and Sample Student Work

©2013 The Foundation for American Christian Education

PART III

THE HAND OF GOD IN AMERICAN EDUCATION:

RESTORING THE MIND AND HEART OF A NATION

The Noah Plan®
Biblical · Classical · American Education

The Beginnings of The Foundation for American Christian Education and Its Founders

Verna M. Hall, out of concern for her beloved country, America, began her research into the foundations of America's Christian history in the 1930s. She sought to understand why we continued to slip down the path of socialism. Her answer came when she began to study the original founding documents and papers of the colonial and constitutional periods— the sermons of our founding clergy; the correspondence and public writings of our patriots, and the founding documents of our statesmen. Verna Hall discovered the Providence of God in history and learned that America was the fruit of the westward course of the Gospel of Jesus Christ, establishing on the North American continent a Biblical form of civil government, so that the life, liberty, and talents of the individual might be free to glorify the Lord.

In the 1960s, Christian educator Rosalie J. Slater joined Miss Hall in the effort to discover why Christian educators no longer included the study of America's Christian history and government in their curriculum. This research birthed the Foundation for American Christian Education. Miss Hall and Miss Slater soon learned that the Biblical and historical documentation of America's Christian history had been removed from American textbooks, and, to their dismay, that America's historic methods of Biblical reasoning and writing had been replaced by workbooks and collective programs of study; such as language arts and social studies. Miss Slater restored to the curriculum the integrity of classic literature, composition, English grammar, history, government, and geography as individual subjects. Through her courses of study and syllabi, which introduced to teachers and students key individuals whom God had used throughout history in all fields of learning, Miss Slater restored to American Christian education a Principle Approach® to teaching and learning which had characterized America's education during its founding years.

An American Christian curriculum established upon the understanding of America's Christian history begins with *Teaching and Learning America Christian History: The Principle Approach.* This volume was written as a companion and guide to Miss Hall's book, *The Christian History of the Constitution of the United States of America,* Vol. I: *Christian Self-Government.* The Principle Approach restores the application of America's Biblical and gov-ernmental principles of Christian character and self-government—first, to the individual American citizen, and secondly, to individual subjects. Only as American Christians accept the responsibility for stewardship of our nation's Christian history can we continue to be a testimony of the Hand of God and a light to all nations.

The mission of the Foundation for American Christian Education is to publish and teach America's Christian history and method education by Biblical principles to restore Christian self-government and character to the individual, to families, to churches, and to the nation.

©2013 The Foundation for American Christian Education

Founders

Verna M. Hall

If the foundations be destroyed,
what can the righteous do?
Psalm 11:3

At her first awareness of America's decline and degeneracy, Verna M. Hall began research that led her to know the cause was not economic or political, social, or even moral—but *spiritual*. Willing to lay down her life and focus entirely on God's call, she compiled and published and taught everyone who would listen. This resulted in a still growing mountain of testimonies of changed lives and ministries spawned to restore Christian character to our nation. When the Lord took her home, she was compiling a series on *The Biblical Foundations of the Constitution*, to include the "root," the "fruit," and the "restoration" of America to its providential purpose in God's plan. She was a master builder, hearing from the great Architect, and faithfully laying to the plumb the foundation stones for America's next generation of statesmen. The Foundation for American Christian Education is dedicated to continuing to build true to the design God imparted to Verna Hall.

Rosalie J. Slater

For other foundation can no man lay than
that is laid, which is Jesus Christ.
I Corinthians 3:11

From the moment she first glimpsed Verna's "big red book," God called Rosalie Slater out of a secular doctoral program in education to partner with Verna Hall and to teach the "answer program" for the restoration of America. She gleaned in Miss Hall's rich compilations of early American history the historic method of Biblical education that produced Gospel liberty and Christian civil government. She restored that method which she named "The Principle Approach®" to American Christian education. Together they established the Foundation for American Christian Education, which produced endless testimonies glorifying God, now reaching to a third generation of families in America and other nations. Her vision is to see the Bible as central to all areas of learning and free Americans to be once again self-governed under God. She continues to preside over the Foundation and to write, develop curriculum, and mentor master teachers and parents.

©2013 The Foundation for American Christian Education

The Fruit of an American Christian Education and Its Ideals

The Noah Plan curriculum was developed and tested at StoneBridge School in Chesapeake, Virginia over the past seventeen years. StoneBridge School is a F.A.C.E. demonstration school and the site of Session I of the International Apprenticeship Program.* It is for these reasons that statistics were collected from StoneBridge High School's 1996–1997 senior class.

"StoneBridge High School is an American Christian high school founded on Biblical principles of scholarship, character, and personal self-government. The high school, which is A.C.S.I. accredited, has a particular nature and mission that sets it apart from other Christian high schools in America.

"The rich curriculum and methodology of the full high school program are based upon the Principle Approach of American Christian Education and the Notebook Method, which provide students with the tools and habits of lifelong Christian scholarship and learning. Students are trained to seek God's Word and research primary sources. They are taught the principles of logic in thinking and reasoning and required to relate Biblical principles to their assignments, as well as to their own lives. Extensive essay writing, research papers, science projects, portfolio projects, and the research, writing, and oral defense of the High School Thesis enable these graduates to reason from cause to effect and competently communicate ideas and principles. Juniors are required to complete an apprenticeship in missions or the marketplace, while graduating seniors travel and teach abroad.

"The classic curriculum is historic and Biblical in nature. Advanced Placement (AP) courses are offered in U.S. history, government, calculus, and physics. Combined with a strong foundation in America's Christian history and government, literary classics, the sciences, math, classical and modern languages, and the interdisciplinary study of the fine and performing arts, the students successfully compete with their peers around the nation for college entrance and scholarship awards. The learning success of each student is supported by small classes, a tutorial emphasis, and by the mentoring process that encourages close student-faculty interaction.

"The graduates are prepared to enter a world of diverse challenges and trained to be leaders among their peers. They are equipped to so focus their minds on subject mastery, discipline their bodies for athletic success, apply their hearts to loving the Lord and helping their neighbors, that they might be 'called out' of their generation by God to help solve, not add to, the problems of our times as statesmen and ambassadors of Christ." (Elizabeth L. Youmans, *School Reference Guide: "A School in a Binder,"* StoneBridge School, Chesapeake, Virginia, 1995)

Ideals:

1. "To know God and Jesus Christ, which is eternall life, Joh. 17.3. and therefore, to lay Christ in the bottome as the only foundation of sound knowledge and Learning." *(New Englands First Fruits,* Harvard College, 1648)
2. To bring into captivity every thought to the obedience of Christ (2 Cor. 10:5), therefore building the foundation of Christian liberty (John 8:32).
3. To honor parents and be prepared to build a Christian family where government and education are taught and practiced.
4. To be made complete and adequate, able to fulfill the calling and purposes of God for his life (Hebrews 13:21).
5. "To develop a wise and virtuous man, fit to be trusted with the liberty of his country" (Sam Adams, Colonial Patriot).
6. To be found capable of being an independent scholar, able to articulate a defense of the faith, and to apply Biblically-based and governmental principles, thus prepared to take dominion of domestic and civil responsibilities.

* Teacher Training is now offered through The Slater Institute; see web page at www.face.net.

©2013 The Foundation for American Christian Education

The Noah Plan® Commitment

Every student is uniquely precious to the Lord and to us as parents or educators. We believe that each one is chosen and placed in our care for eternal purposes. Therefore, we agree to the following sacred commitment:

1. **The Noah Plan Is Committed to the Spiritual Growth of Our Students.** We are committed to developing the spiritual stature of our students, bringing them up in the nurture and admo-nition of the Lord unto the fullest respective stature their tender years afford. The Biblical Principle Approach® does not just integrate truth into the subject content, or "tack on" a Christian appearance—it approaches the subject assuming that all knowledge is the knowledge of God and then identifies the principles of the subject that reflect that knowledge, whether it is in algebra, phonics, basketball, or study habits. All of our curricula and methods cultivate our children unto full spiritual stature.

2. **The Noah Plan Is Committed to Academic Excellence.** We are committed to academic excellence, cultivating the fullest expression of the individual through instruction, inspiration, and consecration in intellectual, physical, and artistic pursuits. This is accomplished in the classroom by establishing excellent standards, an enlightened curriculum, and by the practice of reflective learning, Biblical reasoning, writing, and reading. The tutorial emphasis allows every child to learn by receiving help or enrichment as needed. In athletics, art, orchestra, drama, speech, chorus, as well as in every academic subject, we call for the ***Standard of Christ*** in whom resides all excellence.

3. **The Noah Plan Is Committed to Character Development.** We are committed to the character development of every student, bringing to bear the discipline and conviction of Christian self-government. True Christian character is a thing of great beauty and value. All the spiritual knowledge, academic achievement, or athletic prowess in the world cannot succeed without a character molded and strengthened by truth unto usefulness. We design classroom procedures, teaching methods, policies, discipline techniques, athletic programs, and dress code with this goal in mind. Our curriculum is filled with models of great character which inspire and offer vision to our students. We encourage the concern of a community of parents unified by common values and ***principles for mutual support.***

4. **The Noah Plan Is Committed to Leadership Skills for Service.** We are committed to cultivating leadership skills for service in the next generation. Leadership is serving! We envision that every student will learn to reach outside himself or herself to offer a unique contribution to the Lord, becoming others-centered, and taking a responsible place in God's greater purposes.

©2013 The Foundation for American Christian Education

Introducing *The Noah Plan*® Audio CD Contents

Disk 1

Part I

A. INTRODUCING THE NOAH PLAN®
The Editors
The Program Notebook
The Noah Plan Components
How to Use The Noah Plan
Principle Approach® Education
The Seven Biblical Principles of Government
Gaining a Christian Philosophy of Education
Principle Approach Distinctives Effect of Principle Approach Education
Origin of The Noah Plan Curriculum

B. BUILDING CHRISTIAN CHARACTER
Education Defined Biblically
Classroom Routines and Methods
The Notebook Approach
The Four R's
Using Principles and Leading Ideas
Practicing Christian Scholarship
Study Habits
Character Qualities Produced
Developmental Principles of Learning
Literature and Bible Character Studies
The Classroom Constitution
Loving Relationships

Part II

A. TEACHING REFLECTIVE LEARNING
Qualities of Reflective Learning
Tools and Textbooks
The Bible as a Reader Program
Key Word Studies
The Fine and Performing Arts
Celebrating the Curriculum
Portfolio Projects
The High School Thesis
Effective Communication
High School Apprenticeship
Essay Tests
Fact Boxes
Field Studies & Christian History Tours
Visiting Scholars and Artists

Disk 2

Part II (continued)

B. DESIGNING THE WHOLE CURRICULUM
Curriculum Defined
Designing Curriculum
Using Primary Sources
Classic Literature
Composition
Modern and Classical Languages
The Fine and Performing Arts
The Teacher as the "Lively Textbook"
Teacher Notebook Setup
Conclusions

Part III

A. THE NOAH PLAN HIGH SCHOOL
"The Fruit of a Principle Approach Education"

B. STUDENTS DESCRIBE THE HIGH SCHOOL PROGRAM
"High School Apprenticeship"
by Will Brown
"High School Thesis"
by Elizabeth Lundquist
"Senior Trip"
by Joe Kennedy
"High School Portfolio Project"
by Joshua Kennedy
"The Fine and Performing Arts"
by Melody González

©2013 The Foundation for American Christian Education

CPSIA information can be obtained
at www.ICGtesting.com
Printed in the USA
BVHW010843260720
584505BV00004B/22

9 781935 851080